read 1/17

REREAD

Landlord by Design: 9/22

Complete Guide to Residential Property Management

by

Michael P Currie

Landlord by Design:

Complete Guide to Residential Property Management

1st Edition: © 2016 Michael P Currie

This book was published by Landlord by Design

www.landlordbydesign.com

TABLE OF CONTENTS

INTRODUCTION

"All of your dreams can come true if you have
the courage to pursue them." —Walt Disney

I want to start by painting a picture.

You read books, went to seminars, talked to other investors, did your research, and realized that real estate investing is a great path to getting wealthy.

You decide to take action and buy an income property.

So, what now? From all that you've read, you figure that you just kick back, relax, and let the rent checks roll in. You have other people pay down your mortgage while your property increases in value. It couldn't be any easier.

Then it happens. First, you get a call for a plumbing issue. The plumber you carefully selected for your team is busy or out of town. The tenant sends you a text every hour to ask when they're coming to fix the problem. Now, not only do you need to find a plumber ASAP you're also likely in the middle of spending time with family. You may be there for your family physically, but mentally, you're somewhere else.

You solve the issue, and all is right with the world again. The next day, you're having a hard day at work and you get an email. A tenant is putting in notice. They're on a month-to-month lease, so they're only giving you one month to find, screen, place, and turn the apartment. While you're writing up your brilliant rental ad, you decide to check your online banking and you notice a rent check from one of your tenants has bounced.

All of a sudden, the glamour and prestige of being a landlord is starting to wear off. You wonder if it could be you. Are you doing it wrong? I mean, you crunched your numbers; you have positive cash flow. How could you be so off on your expectations?

That's where *Landlord by Design* comes in.

Most real estate investment authors write in extremes. They write either horror stories (which, fortunately, are rare) or hero stories (which, unfortunately, are also rare).

1

The reality is that the lifestyle of the small landlord is a bit of a grind.

You will have to feed your property to cover capital expense. A year's worth of cash flow can be wiped out with one major problem.

Even if you hire a property manager, you'll have to manage them. You won't always agree with them, and, at times, you may think they're not doing enough or taking too long to fill a vacancy.

Here's a reality check. Real estate investing is an amazing way to build wealth, but (and it's a big but) real estate investing is a business. It's also a long-term wealth builder. That's what also makes it great. If you have a good property in a good location, filled with great long-term tenants, and your building is in great shape, then it can actually be a pretty boring easy business.

The challenge is that unless you go into it with a lot of cash in the form of a big down payment, or build something new, it can take one to two mortgage cycles (5 to 10 years) to get to this position. Most the books don't tell you that.

Landlord by Design can help by providing real-world stories and education about property management.

Our mission is to educate and help small landlords and property managers. We tell the truth, which you can't find in books being sold by people trying to glamorize the residential rental business.

We believe that armed with the right knowledge and expectations, people can enjoy life and create wealth at the same time.

It's not a business for everybody, and the income is definitely not passive.

We hope you will find the stories and advice in this book helpful and will keep this book as a "how-to" reference guide to designing your landlording or property management business.

Mike & Shelly Currie

Landlord by Design

CHAPTER 1 - SETTING THE STAGE

"All the world's a stage and most of us are desperately unrehearsed" – Sean O'Casey

What Is a Landlord?

The term *landlord* refers to a person or corporation that owns a house, condominium, townhouse, apartment, garage, land, storage space, or any other kind of real estate that is rented or leased to a person, persons, or business. The person, persons, or business is referred to as a tenant or lessee. Landlord can be interchanged with the term *landlady*.

The history of the landlording business can be traced back to the beginning of societies. It is one of the oldest business models on the planet, yet it hasn't changed much over the years.

I don't know of any places on earth without any rental market.

That makes the entry point and skill level of this business very low. All you need to do is own a form of real estate.

This can be a problem, and the reason why the rental market is inconsistent and generally based on the living and working conditions of the surrounding area of the real estate being rented/leased

What Is Property Management?

Property management is the business of operating, controlling, and overseeing of real estate. Property management can be carried out by one person or a team at a property management company.

The property management person or company will usually be responsible for collecting rent and making sure the property or land is being used for its intended use and maintained properly.

The property manager (individual or company) will also likely offer additional services to lease/rent the space, screen/qualify tenants, pay utility and other bills, produce accounting reports,

3

keep track of revenue and expenses, or act as a project manager for renovations.

The property manager or management company will be the controlling representative of the property and will take action in what they perceive as the best interests of the landlord.

Superintendent or Resident Manager

The superintendent or resident manager is a person or persons who will generally take care of the cleaning of a building's common areas and vacant apartments. They may also do things like show apartments to potential tenants, collect rent, mow the lawn, shovel snow, arrange for maintenance and repairs, and may even do some small repairs. They're hired to assist the property manager or management company, and usually do the job in exchange for a free or almost-free apartment to live in.

What Makes the Perfect Tenant?

The perfect tenant can mean different things to different people. What I consider to be the perfect tenant might be completely different than what someone else might think.

I think, from a basic level, a perfect tenant may be described as someone who pays the rent early, never complains, and lives in the rental for a very long time.

On the surface, that sounds pretty good, and perhaps that could be the exact type of tenant you either have or would like to have.

Now, what I want to do is make you think a bit broader. The landlord/property management business is a people and lifestyle business.

I believe you need to find people who are the right fit for the property you're renting. You cannot judge someone or discriminate against a person or family who wants to rent from you, even though it could be the wrong fit, so I'm not suggesting you violate basic human rights. However, if a person rents from you and it's inconvenient for them to get to work, or visit parents or children, they will likely not stick around.

If someone is a nonsmoker, they'll likely not last long in a building full of smokers. Even if they agreed to compromise to get a choice location to live there. They could be paying the rent on time and not complaining to you, but they would certainly not be the ideal tenant.

Shelly and I owned a condo many years ago, and we had to adjust to some of the comments made by a lot of the elderly residents. We were young, so many assumed we were renters, and many owners didn't like the idea of renters. It wasn't until I joined the condo board and got to know the type of people I was dealing with that they lightened up.

I had to mediate whenever they started talking about what they thought were major crimes against the management, things such as parking in the wrong spot, putting a bike on a balcony, or putting flowers on a balcony.

I had a situation once when I placed a quiet tenant who liked to go to bed early in a semi-detached house, where the tenant on the other side liked to play music and drink. She would complain nonstop right until she moved out. The tenants on both sides paid the rent on time or early, but it wasn't until this particular tenant moved out and another tenant moved in who didn't mind the music that we were able to get peace.

Are tenant complaints always bad? I would argue that if something mechanical is failing or leaking, I would prefer the tenant tell me about it, rather than leaving it. If a roof is leaking, it's better to know sooner rather than later.

Having open communication with your tenants is critical to maintaining long-term relationships with them. I would prefer a tenant tell me about a problem than leave because it bothered them. The problem could include the personality or actions of one of the other tenants in the building. As I mentioned before, it's truly a people business. You need to provide a safe, peaceful environment for all your tenants.

Would the ideal tenant do their own repairs? Yes, if they're good at it.

We have had cases where the tenants did their own work on the property. We've had many cases where carpenters have rented from us, and they end up doing maintenance work for free, or they ask for the supplies to be paid. We also have several tenants who love to garden and do yardwork.

Although these types of tenants are awesome, you cannot expect all tenants to do something around the rental. Most people rent, so that they don't have to do anything.

You shouldn't expect anything over and above what is written in the lease. If you do get someone who does go over and above, make sure to thank them.

I also want to note that buildings themselves, the areas they're in, and how they're managed can attract a certain profile of tenant.

It would be unlikely that you will find working professionals in a rundown building. It would be just as unlikely that senior citizens move into a student rental property.

If a building is in an affluent community, that's more likely the type of client it will attract.

It's important to answer any questions about the area or property honestly.

Is it possible to attract the perfect tenant?

I'll elaborate more in the section on writing an ad, but the short answer is: yes, you can. When you're renting a space, realize that the tenant is going to be looking to rent for lifestyle. Describe the area features and benefits of living there. You need to be aware that bad tenants often seek out unsuspecting amateur landlords. Bad tenants know that big property management companies will do a proper screening, so they will often look for independent landlords. I've found that using lines like "references required with all applications" will scare off some unsavory people and also indicate that you're going to screen them. I'll explain more about red flags later in the book.

I believe that what makes the ideal tenant goes beyond just the minimum standard of paying rent on time and sticking around.

It's a business relationship, and all good business relationships are built on a basis of mutual trust and understanding, plus they absolutely need to pay the rent on time and not cause drama in the property, just as the landlord needs to provide a clean, well maintained place to live.

What Tenants Say About Landlords & Property Managers

I figured I would start this book with the most important part of your business. The tenant. The tenant is the customer. Tenants provide the income or revenue, all of it. Without the customer/tenant, you don't have a business.

I find that many landlords will sometimes complain about their tenants. They forget about the importance of having great tenants.

I wanted to make this section all about the tenants' perspective, this section is all about the kinds of complaints and feedback we've had from various tenants over the years.

My goal with this section is for landlords/property managers to read it, and, hopefully, it will open up a line of communication between the two parties before they enter into a business relationship with each other.

Communication – I think any great relationship rests on communication. We've all heard stories of what happens when communication breaks down. I need to make it clear that, as a landlord or property manager, you're the professional, so it's up to you to initiate the communication.

I talked to a student housing property manager who said she has to make it clear that rent is due on the first of the month. You see, in her experience, if a person is unfamiliar with leasing or living on their own, and comes from a different city or part of the world, they don't know. This particular property manager learned this the hard way very early in her career. She used to assume everyone knew to pay rent the first of the month, which led to frustration and late rent. Now, the rent is on time (unless there's a bigger problem).

I've talked to several tenants who told me stories of how their landlord/property managers didn't respond to emails, texts, or calls. They had to make several attempts to reach the landlord, then when they did, they were slow to respond. When the landlord eventually did respond and fixed the problem, they often suggested that the problem was the tenant's fault. I heard from one tenant who told me how their window fell off its tracks, and the landlord blamed the tenant for breaking it.

Lease explanation – We've heard feedback from many tenants about the lease. I was surprised to find out that many tenants never signed a lease agreement or received a copy of their lease. If they did sign a lease, it was never fully explained to them what they were signing.

This lead to them not knowing when and how to give proper notice, when the rent was due, how they were expected to pay, who to call in case of an emergency, how long the lease was for, what the rules of the property were, and whether or not they were allowed to have roommates or to sublet.

They didn't know what was included or excluded from the lease; things like garbage removal, lawn care, and snow removal; what utilities were included or excluded such as electricity, natural gas, oil, water, and hot water; and where to park (if parking was included).

They didn't know about extra charges for lease violations or additional services, including late payments, parking, extra parking spaces, lost keys, lock out, and non-sufficient funds (NSF). It's up to the landlord/property manager to communicate these to the tenant.

Access to the unit – This is a cause for complaints from many tenants. The communication seems to be limited. Many landlords/property managers appear to forget that the rental unit is someone's home and not just a commodity. As a culture, we like to have notice before anyone enters our home, so, at the very least, we can shove stuff under the bed or in closets. I feel that, based on tenant feedback, we need to be conscious of this fact, so unless it's an emergency, it's a good idea to give as much notice as possible. All landlords should also explain the rules and expectations of entry at the lease signing.

Security/damage deposit – If you're collecting a security deposit, you need to explain why and how much it's for. Tenants often complain that landlords don't provide an explanation or tell them what's required to get it back. We often have tenants who think it's a cash grab at the end of tenancy. The reason for that is, generally, because of a lack of communication when the deposit is collected.

Residential tenancy guide, building rules, and/or links to websites will provide the information – in many regions, landlords are required to provide the residential tenancy guide at every lease signing.

The lack of education on the lease agreement leads to uncertainty, and, in some cases, to disagreements. If a relationship fails between a landlord/property manager and tenant, it can usually be traced back to the lease signing.

Not taking maintenance complaints seriously – We've heard feedback from many tenants about the unwillingness of their landlord/property managers to take a look at problems. In our experience, if a tenant complains about a window leak, it's important to address the problem quickly. Even if you don't think it's a big deal, water damage can become a big deal over time, and, if the tenant leaves, you'll need to fix it before the new tenant moves in. We also notice that after a new tenant moves in, there are often things that break or leak, no matter how long the previous tenant lived there. That can happen for a number of reasons, the main one being that the previous tenant may have lived with a light switch that didn't work, an electrical outlet that didn't work, or a creaky or sticky door. Then when the new tenant arrives, they want to both have the problem fixed and test the response time of their new landlord/property manager.

Another reason could be that with new users of appliances, things work differently and break. We've had many tenants say they moved out of places because they couldn't get the landlord/property manager to fix anything. We've even heard stories about landlords/property managers saying they were going to fix, repair, or replace things before a tenant moved in, and then not doing it. I interviewed one tenant who was paying big rent in a newly renovated condo. The problem was, that some of the baseboards, kitchen hardware, and other finish work weren't completed before they moved in, even though the landlord told them it would be all done before they moved in. Now, he has to chase his landlord to finish the work (four months after he and his girlfriend moved in). The unfortunate part is that he's looking at options to get out of the lease and move to a finished space. This landlord will have to either actually finish the work or make empty promises to the next tenant.

Not taking complaints about other tenants in the building seriously – Nothing will clear out a building quicker than a terrible tenant. It could be that they're in everyone else's business, they play their music too loud, fight with a spouse or children, walk with heavy feet, or any number of reasons. It's important to listen to complaints about them, and talk to the complainer and the person being complained about. Listen to both sides of the story. Is the complaint legitimate? The complaints may not be realistic, especially if the building has thin walls, or the wrong tenant mix. If a teenager lives in an old age home, it may not be realistic for the teen to complain that the old people want silence after 9 p.m. If you're a tenant moving into a particular area or building, check out the neighborhood at various times of day, before you sign the lease. Make sure the building is the right fit for you; however, if it turns out that your neighbor is a drug-dealing crackhead, you need to make the landlord aware, and if they don't take the complaint seriously, then make sure to complain to the local tenancy authority.

We took over an apartment building once and quickly found out we had a bad apple. Unfortunately, we lost two tenants before we took action. The person who was being complained about was the superintendent, so when we confronted him, he came up with a great story about how these particular tenants were jealous that he became the super, and they were trying to give him a bad rap. The truth turned out to be that our super was great when he was sober; however, when he got intoxicated, he was a rowdy belligerent drunk. That was confirmed one night when the police called me to say he was being taken in for having a fight in the lobby of the building with one of the other tenants.

Feeling they need to withhold part or all of rent until maintenance or repairs are completed – We have heard this threat used or action taken by some tenants. I want to make it clear that if you're a tenant, this is a bad idea. We interviewed several tenants who felt this was the only option, but it's not true. If a tenant isn't paying the rent, they're in violation of the basic principle of a lease agreement (whether it's verbal or written). It can be frustrating if a landlord isn't fulfilling their repairs and maintenance obligations; however, both parties need to follow the rules of the local tenancy authority. As a tenant, you cannot withhold rent, and, for that matter, a landlord cannot withhold services if you're late or haven't paid. The landlord can start the eviction process and get you out, but the landlord/property manager cannot do things like shut off the power or water to try to force rent payment. The best solution is to contact the landlord if you cannot pay and try and work out a deal to either pay or move out.

What to Ask When Hiring a Property Manager

One lesson I've learned on my real estate journey is that you cannot do it all. That has led me to getting experience in interviewing, hiring, and firing property managers.

I want to share with you some of my insights. This can be an extremely important subject matter, especially if you buy properties outside of the area in which you live.

When you decide to hire a property manager, they become a trusted advisor and business partner. If you need to micromanage or end up managing the property yourself at the same time you're paying someone to do it, it's not worth it.

I've had experiences where my property manager was causing more problems than they were solving. That cost me more money, time, and gray hair than if I just did it myself.

You need to trust your property manager. They will need to be empowered to make judgment calls that will cost you money, but keep your property maintained and your tenants happy.

Cheaper is not always better. I have interviewed property managers who offered some great pricing; however, they seemed to have a limited network of repair people or strategy to deal with tenant relation issues, tenancy board, or other problems.

I will add that expensive may not be great either. I've spoken to some property managers, who are quite expensive, but still have limited experience and face the same challenges as the super cheap ones.

I know what you're thinking. How does someone like me, who writes, researches, studies, and actively manages properties, even find a property manager who is willing to work for me? I will admit, I do have high expectations, and I'm big on accountability, but I've found that people who want to strive and are passionate about doing a great job will be okay with that.

Here are some questions to ask potential property managers, and the reasons for asking them:

The first question is to yourself: Why do I want to hire a property manager? – When you start out investing in properties, I would suggest you manage your own properties. If you do, it will give you an appreciation for what a property manager does. If this isn't possible, then make sure you ask yourself if you really want to invest in real estate. The reason I say this is because if you're unable to manage the property yourself, it can be a difficult job finding and keeping a good property manager. It can be very stressful and a lot of work managing a bad property manager. One reason I've hired property managers to help with our portfolio is because of the properties being physically too far away to manage. The other reason is to free up time so I could focus on buying more properties, leaving the management to others. My wife and I also manage properties, so that we stay current with all that's involved in the property management business.

Why do you like doing property management? – Property management is a customer-service-based business. It's important that your property manager enjoys dealing with people and has problem-solving skills. If they're not passionate about problem solving and customer service, they will likely not be a very good manager. Retention of tenants is a good measurement of success, you can ask about long-term tenants in units they managed. Ask what they do that makes people want to stay.

What do you do to attract and advertise for tenants? – You will want samples of rental ads. In this book, I talk about marketing and making great ads.

How long does it take you to fill a vacancy – This will depend on a lot of variables; however, I would say if you had to determine an average, it would be 45 to 60 days. This would be shorter in a hot rental market, and longer if it's a very specific type of property, like a high-end house.

Do you have liability insurance? – If you have an income property, your insurance company will likely pick up the tab if you have a problem such as a slip and fall, etc. The challenge will be if you expected your property manager to salt after a snowstorm and they were negligent, which caused the problem. Then, is it fair that your insurance is going to inevitably increase because of your property manager's negligence?

Do you only hire contractors or trades people who are insured? – If your property manager hires a "guy" for cash on the side and he falls off your roof and dies or is injured, you or your insurance company will be picking up the tab if they're not properly insured. It could also be even worse if your insurance company doesn't want to pay the claim at all.

Do you sign legal contracts with contractors? – If the work doesn't get completed by a hired contractor, there needs to be recourse. The property manager should not pay them in full before the work is complete. There needs to be a plan to solve any disputes between the contractor and your property manager. In some cases, an unresolved dispute could lead to an unhappy contractor putting a lien on your property, or you paying another contractor to complete unfinished work.

Do you have any experience managing properties? – I agree that you may have to give someone a chance if they're starting out, but you better have a good reason for trusting an expensive asset into their care. I would not commit to anything long-term with an inexperienced property manager or management company. You will need to monitor them closely. Many property managers usually have experience managing their own properties or someone else's who is close to them before they step out and form a company to manage other people's properties. If they have property management experience, make sure it was with managing a similar type of property as yours.

What is your process for screening tenants? – You need to make sure the property manager has a process to screen tenants that includes a credit check. The best way to avoid a poor experience with a tenant is with tenant screening.

What if the tenant doesn't pay rent? – Your property manager needs to be familiar with local tenancy rules and regulations. They need to have a plan. The plan needs to be very specific.

What was your most challenging tenant relation issue you've ever had to deal with? – You will want to know what kind of issues the property manager has dealt with. If they've never dealt with an uncomfortable tenant situation, they may not know what to do.

Is property management your only job? – Many property managers do other jobs on the side. That can be okay, but you'll want to know how much time they have to devote to property management. Property management can take up a lot of time, and the time of the work can be unpredictable. Are they a professional property manager, or do they just manage property during the downtime while they sell real estate. That can be a problem if they get busy selling houses. I've also seen carpenters and other trades people say they manage properties. They may be great at the maintenance issues, but the customer (tenant) relation issues are the most important part of managing properties.

Do you have any carpentry or handyperson skills? – It can be great if your property manager has the skill to do some of the small jobs. This isn't critical but could be helpful. I will caution you that many carpenters and tradespeople pass themselves off as property managers. The problem is that they often don't have the interpersonal and business skills to deal with the paperwork and various tenant personalities. I'd rather have someone with limited carpentry and other trade skills but great people skills.

What day will you deposit the rent you collect into my account? – This can be very important to you, so you can organize your cash flow. I will tell you that this varies, and sometimes, it can vary based on the size and financial position of your property manager, or the type of building you have to manage. I've had property managers make a deposit by the 5th of the month, the 15th of the month, or the 25th of the month. The date will have an impact on your ability to pay bills. How are they going to deposit your rent money? Will it be by direct deposit, email money transfer, or a good old-fashioned check?

Do you have a background in customer service or sales? – Tenant relations are an extremely important part about managing properties. If they have experience in sales or business of some kind, in which they had to deal with uncomfortable situations with difficult people, it will make them a better property manager. I like to think of it like this: property management is easy, until it isn't. If they've never worked face-to-face with customers, I would be cautious about them having the ability to be confrontational. They will inevitably face even basic situations such as music noise complaints, smoking complaints, loud animals, and loud children. Then there are bigger issues like chasing people for rent, educating them on things like where to put garbage, keeping the property clean, not removing smoke detectors, and many other items. I think you can see why experience in customer service is extremely important for a property manager.

What accounting system do you use? – Accounting is a very important part of property management. Two of the most common small-scale systems are QuickBooks and Simply Accounting. If you're dealing with a large property management company, they will likely have a system that deals specifically with property management. There are several different types of property management software for bigger firms. The property manager will need to provide you with a statement of revenue less expenses, and annual statements. They also need to send you receipts or copies of receipts and invoices for items purchased on your behalf. Do they do the accounting themselves, have a bookkeeper on staff, or use one consistently who is familiar with property management?

Do you have a network of repair and maintenance personnel? Who are they? Can I reach out to them? – If you manage properties, a major key to providing exceptional customer service to your tenants is quickly repairing any problems. If you hire a property manager, they need to have a close network of contractors and tradespeople ready to help. If they cannot provide any specific names or describe them as a team that would be a red flag. They don't have to be on the payroll; however, it's important that a relationship exists. Some key people would be appliance repairer, locksmith, electrician, plumber, carpenter, and general contractor.

Do you live close to where the property is located? – It's important for your property manager to be reasonably close to the properties they manage. They might have someone in the building or nearby, but they personally need to be available in case something bad happens. It would be important for your property manager to be onsite for a flood, fire, major injury, or other major problem.

Do you have references from current and past clients? – It would be a good idea to talk to two people who have properties they currently manage and two they no longer manage. If they're a newer company, they may not have any past clients or ones who have left. If that were the case, I would talk to four current. The interesting part about building owners is that they all have different needs and expectations. That's why you will want to talk to several and ask about what they expect. You could have a client give you a bad review of a property manager, but it might be based on a personal expectation. A friend of mine who has a property management company once told me that he couldn't seem to win. If the units were full and maintenance issues were low, the owners thought he wasn't doing anything but collecting easy money. Then if there were any vacancies and maintenance issues, the owners thought he wasn't doing his job. I think you see the problem.

Summary - I would suggest you email these questions in advance of your interview with the potential property manager. It will be your first test of how good they are at providing customer service. It's best to have a face-to-face meeting, but if that's not possible, then Facetime or Skype should work. When you hire a property manager, it's all about communication. Just as various tenants have various expectations, so do building owners, so you need to be clear with your communication. The property manager needs to be the right fit.

So You Want to Be a Property Manager?

If you're new to investing, I highly recommend you manage at least your first few units. It's a great way to learn what's involved in managing a property. If you're working full time or want freedom, you'll eventually want to hire a property manager. My experience is that proper property management is the most important piece of the real estate investing puzzle. The interesting part is that most of the books on real estate investing that I've read are focused on seeking the perfect property manager. I haven't found very many articles written by property managers about property management.

I've also found that not many property managers are focussed on just property management. A lot of them seem to be real estate agents, contractors, or have another occupation, and they do property management as a sideline.

I find this interesting, since it's an extremely important part of owning investment properties.

I want to make note that we have two great property managers working for us (actually three if you count Shelly and me); however, it hasn't always been that way. We have hired and fired a couple along the way.

When I hired my first property manager, they sold me on the concept of set it and forget it. I felt a sense of relief, but it wasn't until I had a complaint from one of my tenants a few months in, that I started to realize I would have to monitor my property manager.

I've had a few instances of poor customer service provided by past property managers. I might not be involved in all the day-to-day operations; however, we monitor and meet with (usually by phone or email) our property managers on a regular basis.

You may be asking what makes a good property manager. A good property manager is made up of two parts: the people side and the financial side.

If you want to become a property manager for yourself or other people, here are some of the traits and skills you'll need to be great. You'll need to ask yourself a series of questions. If you answer no to most of the following, then please do the land lording business a favor and hire a property manager.

Do you like people? – The love of people will need to be your number one trait. I think this holds true for any customer service position. The interesting part about property management is that you're dealing with people's homes and money. If you're a positive person, you could make a great property manager.

Do you have the ability to take control of a situation? – Sometimes, you have to be able to take control of a situation. If a tenant isn't paying the rent, you need to act (within the law) to solve the issue. Investment properties are small businesses. Listen to the story, then take action. You will likely hear every story possible of how money somehow didn't arrive on time. When you sign up leases, you need to stress the importance of rent coming in on time. The mortgage needs to be paid regardless of the story a tenant tells you. It's your job as a property manager to make sure all rent is paid on time. You need to be in control. My advice is to be fair and firm. For example, if a long-term tenant needs a couple of day's extension after Christmas, it's okay to give it to them. Just make sure they know it's an exception.

Are you a hustler? – Property management is an active job. It requires a lot of effort. When you have vacancies, you need to get them advertised quickly and be ready to show ASAP. Good tenants (customers) have choices. When you get an application, you need to work on getting a tenant approved right away. If a tenant has a maintenance issue, you need to have a solution right away. If one tenant has a problem with another, you need to be ready to defuse the problem right away. Be honest, what pace do you operate at?

Do you have thick skin (or are you easily offended)? – People will push your buttons. We come across all kinds of interesting personalities in the property management business. Sometimes, you may have a personality conflict with one of your tenants; however, you'll have to keep your mouth shut. The tenants are your customers. There's an old retail saying: "The customer is always right." You might be annoyed because you have a tenant complaining nonstop about their neighbor; however, it's your customer. They're paying the mortgage. You need to thank them for their concern and try to work out a deal between them and the tenant they're complaining about.

Do you operate well under pressure? – If you're working full-time and managing properties, imagine your busiest day at work, then imagine a call that a hot water heater blew up while your tenant was out. The rental apartment is flooded, and the tenant is irate (maybe they don't have or cancelled their tenant insurance). They're blaming you, and you need to find someone to replace the water heater and help clean up the mess right away.

Are you a good negotiator? – You need to know or learn how to negotiate. You have to be able to negotiate with tenants, contractors, and, if you're managing buildings for other people, the owners. You'll be in the center of a problem-solving circle.

Are you a sales person? – If you've already acquired buildings, you likely had to sell the idea of becoming a real estate investor to lenders and family. That's just the beginning. If you want to manage properties for other investors, you'll need to sell the value of your services. You'll also need to sell the idea of maintenance and repairs. You need to sell your vacant apartments to your potential tenants (good tenants have choices and need to know why they should rent from you). As a property manager, you will be required to do a lot of selling.

You can learn some of the skills above. As I mentioned in the beginning of this chapter, you should manage your first few properties yourself. That way, when your property manager calls to say you're going to have a vacancy, you know what that feels like. You can trust that your manager is doing everything they can. If you cannot answer yes to any of the questions above, I would suggest you stay away from property management. If you answered yes to some or all of the questions, then maybe you should consider a career in property management or, at least, manage some or all of your own properties.

Many places require specialized training and education. If you're going to become or hire a property manager, make sure that you or they have the right qualifications for your area. Shelly and I are both IPOANS CAM certified. We have the Investment Property Owners Association of Nova Scotia Certified Apartment Manager designation.

Interesting story and real life example of what property management can involve

I had connected with a former property manager the other day, and it got me thinking about some situations that happened at a property she managed for me.

I'm a hands-on guy, and if the police are involved, I'm on the scene. When I think back to one particular night that involved a bit of a showdown with some local thugs, some threats on my life, and the police intervening, I have to say I must have been brave or just plain stupid that night.

I am obviously still alive to tell the tale, so now it's just an interesting story.

Let me set the stage. I had acquired an apartment building that came with a superintendent. I thought that was great; however, my super had a bit of a reputation in the neighborhood for being a drunk who liked to cause trouble with some of the local kids. There was one particular gang of kids who lived across the street. They were what I would call typical teenagers, most of whom had a rough upbringing, and lacked parental supervision. I find sometimes these misguided youth like to band together with other kids in the same situation. I would likely do the same (strength in numbers).

Anyway, I am not really sure and will likely never know who was bullying who, the teens or my super.

What lead to this particular night was a series of situations involving paint balling the entrance to my building, a BB shot through a living room window of one of the apartments (that tenant they picked on, because they thought he was a crack head, It turns out they were right). They also threw a rock through my superintendent's living room window. This all happened over a couple of months.

Well, then one cold February night, I was chilling out at home with my family and I got a call from my super. The kids were at it again. This time, they smashed the living room window of one of my tenants in a lower unit.

It was the straw that broke the camel's back. I got up, jumped into my truck, and headed over to this building. When I pulled up, the kids all ran into the apartment they lived in across the street. I went right over and knocked on the door to get them and come out and explain themselves. I wanted them to stop damaging my building. It was driving me crazy. The kids were holding baseball bats and threatening to kill me. In hindsight, it's probably good they stayed inside. Then my voice of reason showed up. There were actually four voices, and they all had guns. They also had badges and called themselves police.

I'm glad they showed up to defuse the situation. They couldn't do much, but managed to stick around and try to get to the bottom of the situation.

After they tracked down one teen's mother, she talked to her son (who was the ringleader) and everyone agreed to a cease-fire.

I've been in the negotiation business for most of my life and believe that pretty much any situation can be talked out in the light of day. So, the next day, I tracked down the gang of teens to work out a deal.

When I went to their house, they were a bit reluctant to talk; however, as I listened to their story, I started to take their side. They felt that they were being bullied. I basically said, "I understand how you feel; however, the damage you're causing doesn't really affect your bully. It just affects me. The ringleader of the gang was pretty smart and saw my point of view.

In the end, I gave five of them $20 each and made a deal that if anyone damaged my building, they would tell me about it. Then I drove a few of them to a local convenience store so they could spend their cash.

The ringleader was thrilled with the deal, and I never had a problem since that day.

Here's what I learned:

Always keep cool – I often think what might have happened if the police hadn't shown up, or the kids had come outside with the baseball bats, or worse, what if they had a gun? It was really stupid of me to lose my cool; I'm very fortunate that, in the end, the police and the gang of teens were understanding. It could have been worse.

Listen – listen to people. Find out their point of view. The more you listen, the more you learn, and the better you can get along with people.

Negotiate – this is when I realized after all my years in sales, negotiating deals really paid off. If you're not in sales already, I highly recommend a sales or negotiation course. Knowing about human behavior and how to act when confrontation is necessary, is an important property management skill.

The Super Who Was Not Super

We had purchased an apartment building that had a live-in superintendent. I'd met him when we looked at the building, and he seemed like a great guy.

I should have seen the first red flag, which was from the previous owner. He had said that Jim (pseudonym to protect his privacy) was good for showing apartments and cleaning, but I shouldn't allow him to collect the rent or handle any cash.

The day we took over, I got in touch with Jim and set up a meeting. I told him we were willing to honor the previous owner's deal and continue his cleaning service for a rent reduction.

I told Jim that I was going to meet with each tenant individually to sign new leases and find out if they needed any repairs.

My second red flag came when I went to see Jim after my tenant visits, and he asked if anyone said anything about him. I asked him what he meant and he proceeded to tell me how a couple of tenants didn't like him. It was because he stopped the dryers in the laundry room after the designated hours of operation. He also mentioned another tenant who liked to drink and play loud music. He said he had to get after her for disturbing the other tenants. I told him the truth; nobody said anything bad about him. I believed his story. It sounded reasonable.

My third red flag was during the course of our conversation, we were talking about smoking. I told him I wanted to make the halls smoke free and, eventually, make the building smoke free. He told me he had a permit to smoke medical marijuana. He only smoked it by his back window. He also smoked cigarettes occasionally, but not inside.

That night was New Year's Eve. When I woke up in the morning, I had two messages on my phone. The first one was from Jim. He wanted to tell me that he had a fight with the woman he claimed was an alcoholic. He had gone to her apartment to ask her to turn down her music. In a drunken rage, she pushed him down the stairs. He decided it would be best to call the police. He said the police came and it was a bit of a circus with neighbors out on the street and the lady yelling; however, he was able to get it all under control, and he wanted me to know the truth in case someone else called.

The second message was from the accused alcoholic tenant. She left a message to say that she was innocently hanging out in her apartment drinking a few New Year celebration beverages. She said Jim showed up at her door visibly drunk and high. He wanted to come in for a visit and when she declined to let him in, he started yelling obscene things at her. She pushed him back out of the doorway, and that's when he lost his footing and fell down the stairs. Then the lady who lived across the hall called the police.

She also told me not to let Jim fool me. He's actually a mean drunk. He likes to get drunk and fight.

Both messages were long-winded drunken ramblings. I figured there might have been truth in each story, but at this point, I didn't realize the way Jim was. That day (New Year's Day) I typed up a warning letter to both of them about inappropriate conduct. I met with each one separately. They both agreed to a truce and apologized for causing me grief on my first day of owning the building.

Then, about a week later. I was called by Jim to say someone had thrown a rock through his living room window. I thought that was strange. I met with him, and he claimed it might have been retribution for chasing some kids away from the building who were trying to get in and steel fire extinguishers (apparently, some kids find it fun to deploy them at each other). He said it shouldn't happen again, and that everything was good. I had the window replaced.

A week later, guess what? I had a complaint from a lady who lived across the hall from Jim. She claimed he would get drunk and make unwanted advances at her. I talked to Jim about this and he said she was bothering him. He promised he would make sure to stay away from her because he didn't want to lose his job.

Then there was the paintball incident. The same kids paint-balled the front of my building. I tell the story later in this book about how I personally resolved that situation with the kids.

It seemed like at least once a week, I would hear a new Jim story. Unfortunately, since I believed Jim, it wasn't until two really good tenants left that I decided to take action. The theme of all the stories was similar. Jim liked to get drunk, smoke weed, and cause drama. A lot of the tenants in my building and surrounding didn't have cars, and Jim did, so they relied on him for drives, so most wouldn't complain.

I finally had enough. He reminded me of Jim Lahey from the TV show *The Trailer Park Boys* who managed a trailer park. When the owner came around, he would tell her how he had everything under control. The truth was, he was the instigator of most the drama and caused more problems than he solved.

I felt I had the real-life version of Jim as the superintendent of my building.

I arranged a meeting. I had a real "come to Jesus talk" with him. He seemed really sorry and was close to tears. He was on disability for his MS, but said how important it was for him to be able to have some sort of job to keep him moving. He said he wanted to clean the building until he couldn't physically do it anymore (some days, I wasn't so sure he could do it at that point) He said he paid other tenants sometimes to help him clean if he was having a day with a mobility problem.

We had a great chat. He claimed he was going to give up drinking and make sure he didn't cause any more drama in the building.

The interesting part is that he managed to toe the line (we did have the odd chat) until I sold the building. When the new owner took over, I told him the full story and, as far as I know, he's still the superintendent.

The main point I want to make is that you really need to hold anyone who works on the front line with your customers (tenants) accountable for their actions. A bad property manager, superintendent, cleaner, or any other person or company that helps you manage a rental property can damage your business and the building's reputation. If you don't have tenants, you won't have revenue. The job of a building owner is to make sure the tenants are in good hands.

All Property Managers Need This

A property manager toolbox is a crucial piece of equipment for all property managers and landlords. I cannot tell you the amount of times Shelly and I were grateful to have some basic tools with us. I want to point out that we hire out almost all of our maintenance; however, sometimes, if there's an emergency or small repair, we need to have some basic items on hand.

I wanted to write about what you need at all times.

The first step is to go to any local hardware store and pick up a small to medium size toolbox. It should be large enough to carry the items I'm about to suggest but small enough to fit easily in the trunk of your car.

The items I am about to suggest are the minimum; you can carry more, but don't carry any less.

Lock lubricant/deicer – we've gone to show or inspect many properties and the key sticks in the door. With a little bit of lubricant, or in colder climates lock deicer you can avoid a future service call or frustration from your tenant. People won't often do this automatically. I attended a service call one day for a sticky lock, and when I arrived to check it out, I noticed a can of WD-40 in the apartment. The tenants could have easily fixed their own problem; I'm still not sure why they even had WD-40.

Appliance touch up paint – Appliance touch up paint is one of my favorite discoveries as a landlord/property manager. It can make a stove, fridge, bathtub, sink, etc. look awesome with minimal effort. It comes in a small bottle, and can work wonders on chipped appliances or bathroom fixtures.

60 watt light bulb – this should be self-explanatory.

Set of screw drivers – When it comes to carrying screwdrivers, it's a good idea to get a decent variety. If you only want to buy a few, then I would at the very least have a mid-sized Phillips, a small flat head, and a small Robertson or square head. The Phillips screws are very common in door locks and cupboard hinges.

Vice grips – If you're only going to carry one set, a medium pair will do.

Adjustable wrench – medium size

Measuring tape – it will be common for you to have to measure a room, or blinds, appliances, etc.

Channel lock pliers – these can be used for a variety of things.

Needle nose pliers – medium size

Hammer – hammers always come in handy.

Nails – I recommend a couple of sizes, and a small variety of screws is good to have also.

Duct tape – duct tape can be used to temporarily repair just about anything. Make sure to buy the higher quality brand name kind.

Pen – you need to always be ready to take notes,

Pencil – make sure it is sharpened.

Note pad – you can get a small one from a dollar store.

Black Marker – a fine point one is best.

Plastic tie wraps – these are good to hold just about anything together.

Hose clamps – 4″ is good to have for dryer vents, I would also recommend a few small ones; they can come in handy for plumbing repair.

That sums up the basic list for a property manager or landlord who just needs enough for emergency repairs or small repairs.

Why People Hate Being Landlords/Property Managers

We've been real estate investors, landlords, and property managers for several years.

We do a lot of consulting with new, aspiring, and prospective landlords.

We often see a common theme with small landlords. They like the idea of owing properties, but they don't like being landlords.

We hear all sorts of negative tenant stories, plus stories of property managers not living up to their expectations. We often feel that the resentment, pain, and suffering of being a landlord can be avoided or at least minimized with a slight reality check and expectation evaluation.

The number one question we ask anyone who is or wants to be a landlord is Why?

Why do you want to own a property or several properties?

The next question is what?

What do you want to accomplish in your life by owning a property or several properties?

You see, it's important to realize that real estate is only one of many ways to build wealth; there are also several ways to get involved with real estate investing.

The most basic form that I want to discuss is when you buy a property and place it for rent.

It sounds simple and, for the most part, it really is. So, the question is:

How does this simple form of investing get so complicated in the minds of so many small landlords?

Small business realization– When you own an investment property, most people don't seem to realize they own a small business. You bring in revenue, you pay expenses, you pay taxes, you pay vendors to help you maintain it, and you have one or more customers. Small businesses require effort to provide a great product and please your customer (tenant); they're the revenue portion of the business. When we consult with small landlords, this is one of the first things we discuss. Many people don't have the desire to work a regular full-time job, and then have to look after another business when they're off.

Cash flow myth- Many new landlords are under the impression that you can buy a property with a small amount down, place a long-term tenant who's going to pay maximum rent, never have to do any repairs and maintenance, and, viola, they just increased their income by $500 (often less) per month. I agree you should never buy a property without the intent of cash flow (some people buy money-losing properties for tax reasons; I feel if you're in business, you should desire to make money). The reality is that even if your property is cash flowing really well, an eviction, major capital project like windows, roof, etc. or an emergency issue like a sewer backup etc. can wipe out a couple of years of cash flow pretty quickly. If you have an investment property, it's important to set up a contingency fund and a long-term maintenance plan. A lot of investment books seem to focus only on cash flow. Cash flow is important, but it's meaningless if you're constantly stressed out about how you're going to pay for maintenance, repairs, vacancy, etc.

Not knowing whom to call – This can be a major problem and can cause a lot of stress. Picture this: It's a nice sunny afternoon in August; you're having a picnic with your family on a beach an hour outside of town. Then your phone rings. It's one of your tenants and their oven isn't working. They tell you a story of how they need the oven fixed right away because they plan to bake bread to feed the homeless that evening. What do you do? You need to have a plan already in place. If you don't have a plan, it could ruin the rest of your afternoon. In the customer service business, if you don't have the confidence to get it fixed or come

28

up with an alternate plan for your tenant, not only will you cause yourself stress by not being able to fix the problem right away but also the tenant may make you wear their problem. I'll give you an example of how a plan works; this is a true story. Shelly was away in the Caribbean a few months back. She received a text from a tenant whose oven wasn't working and was about to make supper. Shelly sent a text to our appliance repair person. He sent a text back to say he'd be on it ASAP. She followed up with her tenant to let her know the appliance person would be coming and the tenant texted back to say that he had already been there, replaced the oven element, and was gone. I'm not suggesting that all our maintenance issues are solved this easily and quickly; however, my point is to have a list of people to call. Make sure you have a relationship built on integrity. Do not nickel and dime people on small jobs, pay right away, be glad you didn't have to do it, and your customer (tenant) will be happy.

Not wanting to spend any money – When you own properties, the one thing I can predict is that no matter how great your plan is, you will need to spend money at inconvenient times. Maybe your car breaks down, a fridge breaks, and a tenant gives notice all in the same week. It can seem like a hassle, and, for the most part, it is. That is okay; it's all part of the business. It's important to realize that things break and tenants move out. If you're going to own properties, you need to be willing and prepared to spend money on them. Real estate investing using the buy and hold strategy is a long-term plan, not a get-rich-quick plan. A good way to look at your portfolio is to think of it as a big unit; sometimes, people feel reluctant to spend money on homes they're not living in. You need to keep your income properties in good condition to attract and retain tenants, and to keep your revenue stream consistent.

Inconvenient timing of tenant calls – We've had several landlords say they cringe when they see a text or email show up on their phone. They tend to not want to deal with any issue, no matter what it is. I agree that there's never a perfect time or place to receive a call, but you need to realize the tenants are your customers and your product is the rental. Whatever the problem is, deal with it immediately. Customer service issues that are ignored don't tend to get better with time. If you're lucky, the tenant will keep bugging you to fix the issue. If you're unlucky, they'll say nothing and then move out, only to leave you with having to fix the problem before you can rent it again. Think long term and build a reputation for excellent customer service.

Not having time or skills to handle repairs – I invest in real estate for several reasons, a couple of big ones are for future financial security, and to design a lifestyle that puts what I value first (it happens to be family). I would suggest that, unless you're a skilled tradesperson, you hire out your maintenance, and, even if you are a skilled tradesperson, don't get in the habit of working seven days per week. If you're a landlord and you plan to work your regular day job and a property maintenance and renovation job in your off hours, of course you're going to feel run down. Hire out the work. Spend time on a Sunday with your family, instead of painting an apartment. I think you get the picture. The other thing is that if you're a "do it yourselfer" and you're not very good, you are actually taking away value from your properties. I've seen a lot of really bad renovations over the years. Don't be cheap; think long term and let the pros do your renovations.

Huge tax benefits – I've met with people who carry underperforming properties in their portfolio for several years, and they claim it's for the huge tax benefits. I'll tell you there are some fantastic tax advantages to owning investment properties; however, I would not recommend buying income (notice the term *income*) properties for the purpose of losing money. You might lose money, but just don't do it on purpose. Consider the tax advantages an added bonus.

Expectation of Passive income – Real estate investing is not a good way to get passive income. I'm sorry that even though the government considers rental income to be passive, it's actually a very active way to make money. You have to work for it. Now, if you have a simple portfolio consisting of one or two properties, it doesn't have to be hard, but it's still not passive.

Property manager is no good – We've had the experience of dealing with several property managers. We've had some great experiences and some not so good experiences. We have come to realize that in order for a property manager to be good, they need to understand our goals, values, budget, and what we want out of the property management agreement and our investment properties. This can mean a lot of different things to many different people. The property manager needs to be on the same page. I will say that if you're going to hire one, make sure they're qualified to do the job. Don't just trust anyone with your properties.

I hope that explains a bit about what you should expect and assume will happen if you're a landlord. Shelly and I love properties and providing excellent customer service. I will admit that even we might cringe a bit when a call comes in at an inconvenient time; however, all we need to do is remember and focus on our long-term goals. Be happy when a tenant calls, build a team, have people ready who can solve a problem for you.

Accidental Landlord

I think to understand what a landlord or landlady is, we should give the terms a definition. Here's what I found on Wikipedia:

"A landlord is the owner of a house, apartment, condominium, land or real estate which is rented or leased to an individual or business, who is called a tenant (also a *lessee* or *renter*). When a juristic person is in this position, the term *landlord* is used. Other terms include *lessor* and *owner.* The term *landlady* may be used for female owners, and lessor applies to both genders" (Retrieved August 1, 2016 from https://en.wikipedia.org/wiki/Landlord, para. 1).

This is a pretty good start, but I feel it should include a few more items such as room, space, garage, and apartment.

On the surface, it's a pretty simple business; a property owner exchanges the use of the property for money, goods, or services.

The same business model has been used for centuries and will likely be used for centuries to come.

The reality is that, as simple as it sounds, once you add people and personalities, it can be a very complicated and stressful business.

I think a big part of that is because not only are you dealing with money and customers, you're dealing with where people live and work. It is a 24/7, year-round business.

The main purpose of this section is to help the accidental landlords. I get a lot of questions from this segment of the business, and I always want to help.

Here's my definition of an accidental landlord:

A person who's renting out a room or apartment in their house

A person who has moved out of town and couldn't sell their house, so they decide to rent it out

A person who inherits a small real estate portfolio of under 5 units

A person who buys a house that has a tenant occupied unit in it

A person who buys a house that is currently occupied by a long-term tenant

Basically, any small independent landlords who don't intend to accumulate large property portfolios

I feel education is the key to making sure landlords follow the rules, attract good quality tenants, and create both a great landlord and tenant experience.

I also feel that these accidental landlords are often vulnerable targets of professional tenants. They also can get taken advantage of by not having a proper lease, or they may provide a poor tenant experience and cause stress for themselves and their tenant.

A poor tenant experience can get a small landlord involved in legal battles, tenancy board, property damage situations, and, of course, lost revenue.

To help avoid some of the above listed experiences, I have compiled a landlord starter kit list (I hope this helps).

#1 Tenant screening, tenant screening, tenant screening – I have already written a lot on this topic, but I cannot emphasize it enough. If you're buying a place that's tenant occupied, you need to know all about the current tenant. Don't trust what the current owner might say. They could be trying to sell their way out of a tenant issue. If you own a vacant space and plan to rent it out, make sure to properly screen your applications. The tenant screening should consist of the following four pillars:

Past and current landlords

Character references

Verification of employment or source and amount of income

Credit check

I often hear a lot of excuses when it comes to not properly screening tenants. I'm going to eliminate your excuse bag and provide some of my personal resources. You'll need to check out your local tenant rules and laws (I don't make any claims for the quality of my resources if you decide to use them). We have all the resources you need on our website at http://www.landlordbydesign.com.

#2 Realize you're running a small business – This can be a good news and bad news situation. If you're a landlord, you need to realize you're a small business owner (congratulations). That means you need to keep track of revenue and expenses. This can help you out in many ways at tax time. Make sure you get advice from an accountant when you're filing your tax return. If you only have one unit, you don't have to get fancy, but you should, at the very least, get a scribbler from a dollar store and write down everything you're spending in relation to your rental unit. Also, write down the revenue and keep your receipts.

If you have a small business, that means you have at least one customer. This is where customer service comes into play. If your tenant contacts you, make sure to get back to them prompt-ly. We get a lot of compliments from our tenants about how quick we are to respond to issues, and about our top-notch customer service. When we consult with landlords, I often find landlords feel as if they're being bothered by their tenants when they bring up an issue. I've had to give several small landlords a wake-up-call speech about how they're a business owner and need to provide a high level of customer service, and yes, it will cost money to hire the right people for the job. As you can tell, we're very customer focused and have little patience for landlords who ignore tenant complaints, do half-assed repairs, or ignore required maintenance.

Tenant turnover costs money; it's one of the most expensive parts of the business. If you provide great customer service, you'll have long-term tenants, which will provide you with a steady income and a more profitable experience.

#3 Know about the residential tenancy act in your area – Every province, state, or country has residential tenancy rules, regulations, and conditions that are designed to help make the tenant/landlord experience great. You don't necessarily need to memorize the act, but you're required to have an understanding and know how to acquire the information. In our home province of Nova Scotia, we're required to provide a copy to the tenant when we sign a lease.

#4 Have a team of contacts you can call for repairs and maintenance - When you are a landlord of any size, sometimes repairs and maintenance are required. Make sure you have some contacts ready to go. What can cause a lot of stress for a small landlord is not knowing whom to call or have any idea how to solve a problem. That can lead to delays and poor customer service. Whatever the issue is, deal with it head on. Make sure to assemble a team. Build a list of contacts you can count on. A prepared landlord is a happy landlord.

There's a lot more to the business, but these items will get you started and headed on the right path.

Life in Multi-Family Is Like Having Multiple Families

I'm not sure if Shelly planned this, but one day, when we were making our plan for the day, a great quote slipped out. Shelly said "Life in multi-family is like having multiple families."

I thought it was a very profound statement. We make plans every day on what we have to do with our portfolio of properties we manage. The interesting part about managing properties is that there never seems to be a shortage of new situations.

After Shelly made this statement, I started to reflect and think about the work we do. Sometimes, we don't realize how many lives we affect every day. When you become a property manager, you're responsible for the safe/well-maintained shelter of several families. This is a really important job. It's also, sometimes, a thankless job. If you expect or require a pat on the back for every late night emergency visit, or how fast you solve a problem with an appliance or plumbing issue, then multi-family property management would not be for you.

It is a job that requires self-motivation and pride in a job well done.

We strive to provide the best customer service possible to all our tenants and show a ton of appreciation to the contractors and trades people who help us out.

When you manage multi-family real estate, you become part of every family. You may not get invited to Christmas dinner; however, at some point, you will be asked to help.

That simple statement, which was a reaction to our "to do" list this morning gave me a feeling of pride and a sense of duty.

Shelly and I truly care about all the lives we touch. I agree that multi-family property management can be challenging with all the people and situations we face every day, but for us, we are happy to be part of multiple families.

Real Estate Investing Is a Lifestyle Choice

Real estate investing is a lifestyle choice.

I was asked what I meant by that statement the other day. So, I thought I would share a recent story. It happened over a Saturday, Sunday, and Monday.

We had an ad placed to fill a vacancy. I was communicating with a potential prospect and set up an appointment to show the apartment on a Sunday morning. I just had to figure out how to fit it into my son's hockey and parade schedule that day. Here's what I did. My wife (Shelly), the two boys, and I headed to the rink. When my son got on the ice, I ran out, met the prospect, showed the apartment, had the tenant fill out the application, and made it back to the rink with time to spare.

I still needed a few more pieces of information to start processing the application, so I couldn't start the screening process right away (I like to start the process right away, especially since good tenants have choices; they could be looking at more than one apartment).

The prospect emailed me the information while we were having supper at my parents. As soon as we finished supper, we rushed home, Shelly put the kids to bed, and I ran a credit check, and started calling references.

We were able to process the application by early the next day (once we got in touch with the references, past landlord, etc.)

I contacted him to conditionally offer the apartment; The condition was that we needed to talk to the current landlord (they had requested we not call the current landlord until they were otherwise approved. He was excited, and we made an appointment for me to go to his current apartment to do a lease signing that next night at 7:00 p.m. (after my regular day job).

Then about an hour later, he called back, and it turns out, he wasn't on a month-to-month lease, but a one-year lease. He was locked in for about four more months.

So, back to the drawing board. I immediately went on Kijiji and reposted the ad as a top ad.

We got another prospect, only this time Shelly agreed to show the apartment.

As a real estate investing and property management team, we have to be on the ball and ready for action at all times. It's important in any family to be on the same page with whatever goals you're working toward.

This was just one story of many that I could share.

I hope this story provides some insight into how we fit property management and real estate investing into our lives.

I often say to those who use the "I don't have enough time" or other similar excuses for not taking action in their lives, to take a good look in the mirror and consider the alternative.

Bonding over Rat Poop

This story is about an experience we had renovating a house that had a previous rat problem.

We bought a 150-year-old house to renovate a few years back. We hired contractors to do the majority of the work. We've found over the years that it's a good idea to get involved and keep a close eye on your renovation projects. What this means is that Shelly and I usually end up doing projects that most people don't like doing.

We'll often do things like general cleaning, taking out garbage, sorting construction debris, painting trim, taking apart and cleaning light fixtures, etc.

Shelly and I consider ourselves lucky to be able to work well together. When we're working on a project, we're always aware that each fixture we clean or garbage bag we fill gets us closer to our life goals.

This particular project was going really well. Then it happened. We had to take on the job of cleaning the cupboards. To set the stage, when we purchased the house, the only residents were insects and rodents. Our plumber had already found a few dead rats while replacing pipes.

That being said, what we found in the cupboards was a bit disturbing. One of the lower cupboards had rat poop stuck to the bottom. We're no strangers to rat or mouse droppings; they're quite common. But, in this case, it was smeared on the bottom of the cupboard.

There was only one thing to do, roll up our sleeves and take action. We took turns scraping. We'll both admit it was pretty gross (even for seasoned renovators like us). We managed to scrape it all off, then we had to sanitize with Spray Nine and bleach, and then sand and paint.

It was a lot of work; however, in the end, it all worked out.

Here's the summary of our experience:

1. Rat poop, in general, is disgusting

2. When you don't really think about what you're doing, it makes a disturbing job a lot easier to do (think of it as chocolate).

3. When you experience something disturbing with your renovating partner, it brings you closer together. We're not going to seek out another experience like this; however, we don't regret the experience.

4. Shelly and I had a special bond before, now it is even stronger.

The Family That Invests Together Stays Together

This section is all about being a real estate investor and what that can mean for family life. Let's face it, owning residential real estate and raising a family isn't always easy. I think the obvious part about owning residential real estate is that your business runs 24/7. I want to give some advice to those who are thinking about investing in real estate. I also want to help people who are already investing; you're not alone. The key ingredient to investing as a family is that everyone needs to be sold on the idea. In my opinion, real estate investing is one of the best vehicles for wealth building; however, it's important to take away the emotion and excitement of owning buildings and realize that it's just one of many paths to financial freedom. It's not for everyone.

Here's my story. Shelly and I talked about getting involved in buy and hold real estate investing long before we actually did it. We had several conversations about how each of us would participate in the business. The great thing about our situation is that we had already worked on several flip properties together before we started the Fort Nova Group with our friend Mike Thibeau.

What we discovered as soon as we started was that real estate investing is a lifestyle choice. If you're involved in a relationship, you both need to have the same vision. You must have a clear goal and be able to support each other. I can remember one time we had two vacancies to fill in the same month and both the outgoing tenants had been there for over two years. That meant both units had to be filled and then fixed up and turned over to the new tenants. We don't like to lose revenue; so, of course, that basically meant it all had to happen within a couple of days.

We had to handle two complete paint jobs and several miscellaneous repairs to get the units ready. The great thing in this particular situation was that, in both cases, the tenants moved out a day early, and it was over a long weekend.

We had Friday, Saturday, and Sunday to get both units ready. This required an all-hands-on-deck approach, so when you have small children as we do, you have to either find babysitters, or one parents while the other works; well, in this particular case, we used a combo of both. We also enlisted the services of a painter and a cleaner; plus, I dragged my father into the mix.

We had to work together as a family, knowing that this work was required to get us closer to our goals. That's why it's so important if you're in a relationship to have the same goal. Then there's no unnecessary tension or arguments. You just do it and accept it as part of the lifestyle.

We managed to get one unit completely ready and the other one 85% ready. I had to get my painter to work around some of the tenants' things to finish the paint job.

We also have circumstances where it is necessary to show apartments on evenings or weekends, as well as deal with problems that arise (on a fairly regular basis). I find it very helpful to be able to talk about our situations with each other. We have great tenants; however, we're always aware that great tenants have a choice on where they want to live. What that means to us is that we strive to provide the best customer service possible. If a tenant has an issue, we want to resolve it ASAP. The situations we need to talk out are the gray area complaints. Those are the ones where the tenant might make something seem like an emergency, but it can wait a day.

The key that has helped us is to build a great team of a general contractor, plumber, electrician, and handyman. We've stayed loyal to our team and provided them with some large jobs, so when we need something small done, they never seem to mind taking care of it. We've been in situations early in our investing career when we had calls from tenants with a problem and didn't know whom to call. That made us feel out of control and fearful. We were able to resolve those issues, but realized we needed to put a plan in place to avoid unnecessary stress.

Here is my summary:

Recognize that real estate investing is a lifestyle.

Recognize that real estate investing is just one of many tools to achieve financial freedom.

If you're in a relationship, both parties must share the same vision.

Recognize that real estate investing is a long-term investment. Focus on the big picture; don't fret or worry about the day-to-day challenges.

Build a strong team of tradespeople.

Remember that your tenants are paying your mortgages; provide exceptional customer service.

Real estate investing comes with several challenges and rewards; we've found that working together has made us stronger as a family. It might get crazy busy sometimes, but we wouldn't have it any other way.

Family of investors

Our first zero-down purchase

CHAPTER 2 – HOW TO ATTRACT THE RIGHT TENANTS

"Learn as if you were going to live forever, live as if you were going to die tomorrow" — Mahatma Gandhi

The most important part about having a rental is attracting a great tenant, a person or persons who will be a great fit with the other people living on the property or in the area. You need to have a strategy to make this happen. The following is our basic recipe for attracting great tenants:

How to Set the Right Amount to Charge for Rent

This can be tough. If you set your rent too low, you can be leaving money on the table, possibly attract undesirable tenants, or just get less cash flow.

You want to be at market, or maybe just slightly below. Having your units full all the time is great, but if you have several units and they're always full, it could indicate that you're not charging enough.

I've had several debates on this with other landlords when I had set the rent after a big renovation. The following list will give you a guide on how to set yourself up for success.

Ask yourself what would attract people to your location (schools, jobs, parks, hospitals, and lifestyle).

Would you live in the space or unit you have for rent?

Call numbers you see on for-rent signs, ask other landlords, and ask a local landlord association to find out what all these people are charging for rent in your area.

Look at the pictures in the ads and drive by the properties to see how yours compares based on first impressions.

Make sure to take note of features such as units with in-unit laundry, parking, storage, yard, more than one bathroom, views. (Do you offer anything that other units in the area do not have?)

Make sure to set a price that's at or just below market rent.

How to Write a Great Rental Ad

A well-written rental ad can mean the difference in finding a tenant quickly and having a vacancy. Shelly and I are continuously tweaking our rental ad procedure. We've tried things that work and things that don't. We've also noticed that sometimes, if the market is hot, even poorly written ads work.

In the past year, we've had the opportunity to try a few new things, and I want to share with you what we've found that works. We were forced into finding creative ways to attract attention to our ads based on market conditions. We don't fully understand why, but the amount of qualified tenants applying seems to have dropped off. It could be the amount of current rental inventory that's on the market, or any number of reasons. The reasons for this aren't really important. What's important is getting our units rented quickly.

When you write your ad, remember that people rent for lifestyle. I've seen many cases where a tenant will sacrifice condition and amenities for location, especially if you're close to a university, hospital, or major employer. It's just as important to describe the features and benefits of the area, as to mention the features and benefits of the rental unit. How will renting from you enhance the tenant's life? Perhaps your pet friendly and live across from a dog park. You could be walking distance from a major university. If you're pet friendly, let people know what kinds of pets you will consider. Do you live in a safe neighborhood? Does the building have any security features? Is your property new or renovated? Is public transportation available close to your property? Is the unit furnished? If it is furnished, is there an option to have it unfurnished? Is it walking distance to any restaurants, gyms, hospitals, schools, or other amenities that might be helpful?

Keywords that show up in searches are important. People with pets, for example, often have a hard time finding rentals, so they may enter words like *pet friendly, dogs, cats,* or similar in the search bar when looking for a unit. Use keywords like the area you're in, not just the city or town. In our area, the university section is the south end, so it would be important for anyone advertising in that area to put *south end* in the ad.

We continuously strive to improve our copy (text). Make sure you're descriptive. Don't be afraid to be creative. Put yourself in the tenant's shoes. Don't assume they know the area and all it has to offer. Saying things like "close to all amenities" won't help your prospects imagine themselves sitting in the local Starbucks or relaxing at the nearby spa. List the local businesses. People are generally looking to move to an area for lifestyle. What are the names of the schools, major businesses, hospitals, etc.?

Be descriptive about the property. Does it have a backyard? Or does it have a large backyard oasis with luscious grass, lots of shade trees, and a perfect spot to place a BBQ? What do the rooms look like? Is it a living room? Or is it a large living room with gorgeous hardwood floors and crown molding? If the property has a dishwasher, make a point of talking about it. You could write something like "no more fighting over who does the dishes," or "never wash a dish as long as you live here." If the property has any special equipment like a heat pump, woodstove, Jacuzzi, or swimming pool, make sure to describe it well.

The first game changer was including a video. When we included a couple of videos in ads, the views increased and the feedback we got from prospects was amazing. A more detailed description of our video experience comes later in this section. The video is especially important if you're trying to attract out-of-town tenants.

The next game changer was from a man who manages a couple of our properties. He made a suggestion that got us immediate results. He said to put something eye-catching, even borderline crazy in the subject line. The object is to make your ad stand out from the hundreds of other ads posted online. Here are some of the lines you can use (depending on the season, or recent events): "Cupid approved," "ghost-free," "zombie-free," "Santa approved," "Guaranteed minion-free." It can be fun to let your imagination run wild. The stranger the better. You just want to get your ad noticed. Don't be afraid to be bold?

Finally, make sure to post lots of pictures. I'm still amazed when I see rental ads without pictures of the inside or outside or very few pictures. People love pictures and lots of them. That's why if you're not able to do a video, you must have great pictures. You want to help your prospect feel what the unit might be like.

In summary, make sure to take your time and write a great ad. Always be bold. Remember what you're trying to do. You need to attract attention to get appointments for a viewing. Then ultimately, you fill your vacancy fast.

Wait Patiently for a Response to Your Rental Ads

We write what we think is a spectacular rental ad. We research our competition and make sure we're asking the correct rent. We place the ad on Kijiji and make it a top ad (the instructions are on top of the web page). Then we wait for the emails to come in.

Well, what happens when nothing comes in? Zero response. The reality seems to be that no matter what rental market you're in, sometimes, for whatever reason, the leads don't come pouring in.

We've had this happen to us in an August with an apartment a short walking distance from a large community college. We've had it happen in various months of the year.

I have to admit, sometimes, having zero leads can be better than being flooded with undesirable leads.

I will also admit that I've had to use some positive self-talk to prevent myself from worrying about the possible pending vacancy.

I believe that when you have a vacancy to fill, you need to hustle. The following steps may not solve all your vacancy problems, but they will surely help:

1. Stay positive; believe that you're going to attract an awesome tenant.

2. Keep your ad current, keep it fresh, and make sure to repost or pay for a top ad to stay visible. Make it easy for potential tenants to find you. If you have zero leads in the first couple of weeks and you're in a strong rental area, review your price and adjust if necessary. Review your description and pictures and modify if needed.

3. Make sure your ad has great pictures and several of them (never post an ad without pictures).

4. Make sure your ad is well written and really describes the apartment, house, or room in a positive way. Describe what's close by and build a case for why someone would want to live there. People rent for lifestyle (to be close to hospitals, schools, major industry, etc.) Write an ad that makes you stand out from your competition.

5. Make sure your vacancy is advertised properly. You need to be online as part of your strategy. We use Kijiji; it's free and very effective in our area. Other sites may work better in other areas. Make sure you're online somewhere. That's how the majority of your tenants will find you.

6. Let the other tenants in the building know you have an upcoming vacancy. We've had some great luck with tenants referred by other tenants. If you have a lot of rental units, offer an ongoing referral program. Some examples might be a $100 gift card, or half month's rent free.

7. When you get a phone or email lead, respond immediately and be upbeat. Thank people for getting in touch with you. Build credibility as a property manager or landlord. Always remember your tenants are your customers. Great customers have choices, so you need to provide the best customer service in your market, which will allow you to attract and keep tenants. I've had many tenants complain that they contacted other property management companies and landlords, but they were slow or didn't respond.

8. When you show the unit, remember, that's your time to shine as a salesperson. Do a proper feature and benefit demonstration. If it does require some work, communicate with your potential tenant what you intend to do before they move in. Have a

plan before the potential tenant shows up. Don't expect that the current tenant is going to clean up and stage the unit for your showing. Arrive early. Remember, when you bought the building. How was it presented to you? Unfortunately, in most cases, you likely had a weak presentation from your real estate agent or the owner. This isn't acceptable in our business. Present the property with enthusiasm. You're selling the benefits of the unit, area, and you.

9. Try to set up more than one showing close together in time. In our experience, unfortunately, only about 50% of appointments show up. Don't get discouraged if your appointment is a no-show. It's a reality we all face in any business we're involved in; it's not exclusive to property management.

10. If you hire someone to fill a vacancy, make sure that they follow the steps above. I've had complaints from people in the past who have contacted people I hired to fill vacancies. They said they were slow to respond to emails and phone messages. It's your investment property, so make sure you hire the right people to fill your vacancies.

How to Make a Youtube Video for Your Ad

I have to admit that Shelly and I talked about this idea for a long time before we took action on it. The concept is simple. I would make a video of Shelly showing the property, upload it to YouTube, and then insert the link into our Kijiji ad.

A few of the barriers or perceived barriers were that we didn't have a fancy video camera, and, since neither of us were particularly tech savvy, we had been procrastinating about buying a special camera and microphone. We also didn't have any vacancies and figured we'd rather video a vacant unit. We were also not sure on what we would say. We talked about writing a script, maybe even hiring a videographer to help us.

Then I found a clip on YouTube from a realtor. In the video, he mentioned that he was using his iPad to film it. I thought, *Wow, the quality isn't too bad, considering it's just the stock iPad camera.*

I made the iPad video discovery around the same time as a tenant of ours moved out early, which allowed us time with a vacant apartment before the new tenant moved in.

Shelly and I decided to take action. We both had a lot of experience showing apartments, so we figured we'd just shoot a video and see how it turned out. We figured that, in the worst-case scenario, we'd find out that videos weren't for us and abandon the idea.

We made the video and placed a link to it in the rental ad. The response was amazing. We showed the apartment to four different people. Each person we showed it to thanked Shelly for making the video. They all mentioned they wished more people would post videos of their apartments. We had the apartment leased within days of posting the video ad.

We now do a video for all of our rental ads. We wish we had done this years ago.

If you're reading this and don't have a YouTube account, make sure to go to YouTube.com and set up a free account. It's easy.

Doing a Rental Open House

When it comes to renting homes, Shelly and I are always trying to come up with new ways to efficiently show places to potential tenants. We recently tried a new idea for us, a rental open house.

I do realize that an open house is not a new concept; however, it's the first one we did.

It worked out really well; we had several people show up. A couple of families were driving in the area, but most showed up because of the ad Shelly placed on Kijiji.

The few days leading up to the open house, we offered a couple of possible times for a viewing, and then if they didn't work she told them about the open house.

It was a great way to show the apartment to several potential tenants at the same time. This also minimized the inconvenience of showings for the current residents.

A couple of the value-added items were Shelly's fresh-baked cookies, sandwich board sign with balloons. Shelly also placed balloons on the house, so people could clearly see which town-house for rent was ours.

Our first open house was a great success, and made us stand out from the other townhouses for rent in the area.

It is an idea that we will be using again for other rentals.

Rental open house

When You Arrive to Show a Unit and It Is Disgusting

I have shown lots of apartments, and I'm happy to say that the majority are pretty clean and in good repair. I've been fortunate not to have had many surprises; however, one showing sticks out in my mind as being the worst ever.

I had posted an ad and had several responses over one particu-lar weekend. I contacted the tenant to give notice for access (alt-hough once a tenant gives notice to quit in Nova Scotia, they have to provide access, even without 24 hour notice). We still like to give as much notice as possible. My tenant said it would be no problem; however, she was away and just her two teen-age kids would be at home.

She said she would contact them and ask them to clean up. I thanked her and planned my showings.

I had three, so I staggered them a half hour apart. I showed up 30 minutes early and was greeted by a friendly teenager. She welcomed me in, and then quickly put on her headphones and got back to her phone and computer.

I was standing in the living room, thinking, *OMG, how am I going to make this place look amazing in 30 minutes?* There was dog hair everywhere.

Pizza boxes and dishes were stacked in the sink. The curtains were closed and the place had a cigarette smell. I walked around and noticed a dirty cat box.

I opened the curtains, started sweeping the floor, and then the doorbell rang. My first showing came twenty minutes early. They were a nice young well-dressed couple. I felt embarrassed to bring them in; however, I figured the show must go on. I could tell by the body language that they weren't very impressed.

We did a tour starting upstairs, and working our way down. The nail in my showings coffin was when we went to the basement rec room and right in the middle of the floor was dog poop. I rushed them through to show them the spacious laundry room, but I'm pretty sure they noticed.

They did take an application, but I never heard from them again.

Once they left, I had about 20 minutes to clean this three level house from top to bottom. I jammed dirty dishes back in cup-boards, swept, and mopped. Fortunately, I brought a few gar-bage bags with me, so I did a sprint cleanup. I even sprayed with Febreze. I'm not going to say the job was perfect, but I have to admit, it was pretty good, considering the mess and what I had to work with. Fortunately or unfortunately, my second appointment didn't show. That gave me time to get it ready for my third ap-pointment.

When they showed up, I just hoped they wouldn't look in the kitchen cupboards (they didn't).

The great thing is that they were very impressed and were well-qualified tenants who filled out an application on the spot.

As you can see, my story had a happy ending. The lesson is to always arrive early for your showings. Make sure to also come prepared with some basic supplies like a broom, dustpan, Febreze, and garbage bags.

I'm not sure what I could have done differently that day. I guess if I could go back in time, I would have arrived earlier, taking into account that teenagers were looking after the house.

How to Respond to Rental Inquiries

This step might sound simple; however, believe it or not, many people either respond slowly or not at all to rental ads. When I was taking a course to become a certified apartment manager, we had an assignment to call around and ask about apartments. We were tasked with calling on ads for apartments managed by big companies and small independent rentals. I was amazed at how many people in the class had a negative experience and how many of the people responding to emails and phone calls provided very limited information, didn't ask qualifying questions, and didn't try to get an appointment for a viewing. I personally experienced property managers who answered the phone as if I were a major inconvenience. I have laid out some simple steps to make sure you answer your ads properly. Customer service is key.

- Quick response is paramount. Make sure it's a priority to respond to your inquiries immediately.
- Use positive language and tone when responding to potential renters.
- Thank potential renters for responding to your ad.
- Ask qualifying questions that don't violate human rights or the fair housing act.
- **Some examples of qualifying questions are:**
    - How many people will be living with you?
    - Where do you work?
    - Do you smoke?
    - Do you have any pets?

     ○ Entice a potential tenant into making an appointment to view the apartment by using assumptive questions such as, "Would Tuesday evening be a good time to view the apartment?"

How to Do a Proper Showing

When you're contacted by a prospect, the first goal is to qualify, if you ask your qualifying questions and the prospect sounds good, your next step is to get an appointment. Don't try to sell the apartment over the phone. Make an appointment. You have a lot better shot at renting your apartment if you can get face-to-face with your prospect. If the caller has a lot of questions, tell them you will answer all of the questions at the showing. The key to success is to make yourself available. Make sure you're flexible with your times to meet with a potential tenant. When we first started showing apartments, we used to get frustrated when people didn't show up. That's a reality all property managers/landlords face. Expect only about 50% to show up and schedule according to that math. I've laid out the following steps to guide you in setting up successful showings:

- It's crucial to make yourself available.
- Set expectations for yourself: My research and experience has shown that 50% of scheduled appointments don't show up.
- Set up several appointments in one timeframe to maximize your time. For example, if you have four people interested in viewing the apartment, set up the appointments on the same day in 15-minute increments.
- Follow up with potential tenant(s) the day of the viewing to confirm their appointment with you.

Showing the apartment is your chance to stand out from your competition. The showing is your product demonstration. Make it exciting. Don't just point out the obvious and say things like "This is the kitchen." Everyone knows what a kitchen looks like. Instead, say, "Since the kitchen has south-facing windows, you get a lot of natural sunlight in this space." Start on the outside of the building. Show them the surrounding area. Remember, people rent for lifestyle, and good tenants have a choice. A backyard,

BBQ area, playground, clothesline, etc. may be major selling points to a prospect. Show all the features and benefits of your rental, both inside and out.

Here's a checklist for a successful showing:

- Arrive early.
- Turn on all lights and open all curtains and blinds.
- Plan your presentation of property and area.
  - Show outside of property first.
  - Show storage area (if any).
  - Show inside of property.
- Include features and benefits of living there instead of just pointing out the obvious.
- Remember that people rent for lifestyle, so continue to mention the features of the area based on your potential tenant's profile.
- Know the approximate cost or how to access the information for the approximate cost of any utilities that aren't included in the rent.
- Have business cards and/or rental information sheet on the unit you're showing.
- Have a pen for the potential tenant to take notes.
- Have a rental application with you and offer the opportunity for the potential tenant to fill it out.

CHAPTER 3 – TENANT SCREENING

"The longer we follow the right path, the easier it becomes" —English Proverb

The Four Pillars of Tenant Screening

Tenant screening is the most important part about being a property manager. We can summarize the screening process into four main pillars:

Credit check

Current Landlord & Previous Landlord

Income verification

References

Never take short cuts or skip any of the four main pillars in this process. The primary reason is that before you've selected a tenant for your space, you have the rights; the tenancy laws are on your side. You're better off with a vacancy rather than a bad tenant.

Once you select a tenant, the tenancy laws work in favor of the tenant to protect them, making it more difficult for you to remove them.

It's assumed that you're a business owner, and that you should know the risks involved in selecting the wrong tenant. So, it's your fault if you selected a bad one. The tenancy boards don't accept excuses from landlords who don't take the business of being a landlord seriously. We're the professionals and are expected to know how to properly screen a tenant, not be reckless, and look out for the well-being of the other tenants and the property.

If you find yourself in trouble and at a tenancy meeting, you need to have excellent documentation to back up your story.

You're required to have a well-written lease, cancelled checks, bank statements, pictures, or whatever you need to state your case.

You're also required to prove that you're consistent in your tenant screening process. For example, if you turn someone down based on a credit rating, you may be asked to provide other credit reports to prove that you ran a credit report on all your potential tenants. You can't just run it on the tenants you feel may be credit risks.

Your process is expected to be fair for all people. It cannot violate any human rights. We'll get into that after we go through the pillars.

Review of the four pillars to a proper tenant screening:

Pillar 1 – Credit Check

This is the most important step in the process. I'll show you why.

I want to plead my case for doing credit checks. I believe you should do a credit check on every single potential tenant. I am aware that it costs money, so I would only check out potential candidates that you feel are going to be great. The credit check is important for a number of reasons. There are two reports we use at tenantverification.com Transunion and Equafax. We don't always have to do both; however, sometimes, it's necessary. The Transunion report is more detailed on the payment history; however, the Equafax report uses a rating system, A, B, C and shows a risk rating based on beacon score. When a tenant fills out your application, they provide information that's sometimes contradicted in the report or is consistent with the report such as previous addresses, number of debts (good or bad), and current or previous employers. I've had some people tell me that I will see a few glitches over the past year on their report, then when I take a look, they have bad history for several years. A credit report is about much more than a beacon score. I've had some property managers tell me, they don't bother to do a credit check for various reasons (excuses) The reality is that now that we're in the information age, there's really no excuse for a property manager to not do a credit check before they approve a tenant.

Here are some of the excuses for not doing a credit check followed by the reasons you should:

I don't want to spend the money.

Yes, it will cost you money, but it can save you money long term compared to eviction, or the aggravation of a bad tenant.

I don't know how to get an applicant's credit report

There are several companies that you can sign up for. Yes, there are some rules around privacy and handling sensitive material; however, it's generally free to sign up with a verification company, and its pay per use with a cost of about $25 per report. I signed up with a company called www.tenantverification.com. This company has worked well for me. If you're a member of IP-OANS in Nova Scotia, you can get credit reports for about $10. If you google "tenant screening," several tenant screening agencies will show up. There, now nobody has an excuse to not get a credit check.

The prospect told me they have bad credit, so I'm not going to bother with a credit report

Here's the deal: the credit report is more than just about a credit score. The report tells a story. Each time a person applies for credit, they enter their current address and phone number. Also, if they have even minimal credit like a credit card, they will have a payment history. You'll be able to tell if they pay their current debt obligation payments on time. You'll be able to see the companies where they applied for credit. The story could be good or really bad. If a tenant has lied about living in a certain place, it may show up. We've had tenants say their previous address was living at home with parents, so they don't have any references. Then you find out the truth that they've lived in five different places in a very short time. Think of a credit report as a way to back up the information on the application.

They have a cosigner, so I'll be safe if they don't pay

The purpose of a cosigner is as a plan B to collect the rent if the tenant stops paying. I want to make it clear that if you take on a cosigner, you need to do a credit check on them too. Make sure they're able to qualify for the apartment, before you make them sign a lease. We have had cosigners who had worse credit than the one applying.

Summary

Those are the main excuses I hear for not doing a credit check. When you do run the report, the credit score is also an important part. A fantastic score (which means very low default rate) is in the 700s. A red flag score would be 550 or less. The lower the score, the higher the chances of default.

I do want to caution you that some cell phone companies will put an unpaid phone bill into default, pretty much as soon as it's just overdue. It could be the only thing bringing down the score. You need to use common sense when you read credit reports.

Like I said, the credit report is only one of the four pillars of successful applicant screening.

Pillar 2 – Current and Previous Landlord Check

It's important to contact the current landlord. When the tenant provides you with the phone number on the application, make sure to google the phone number. If they provide the name of a rental company, google the company and make sure the phone numbers match. We've had situations where a potential tenant will provide the number of a friend, who will pose as a property manager/landlord.

Contacting the current landlord is an important part; however, realize that if someone is trying to get rid of a bad tenant, they might not tell you the truth, so they can get rid of the person.

So, to reiterate, verify the information they're providing the best way you can. Google can be a great help. All you need to do is enter the phone number or the name of the alleged landlord/property manager.

I will point out that it's common for a tenant to not know an exact name and contact number on the spot, especially if they're currently renting from a large organization.

The past landlord is often where you will strike dirt if there was an issue. The past landlord doesn't have anything to gain by lying.

When you contact the current and past landlords, you can ask questions like the following:

Did they pay the rent on time?

Did they have any problems with other tenants in the building?

Were they a clean tenant?

Were they a hoarder?

How long did they rent from you?

Why did they leave?

Did they give proper notice?

The potential tenant may not want you to contact the current landlord/property manager if they haven't provided notice. That might be okay if all the other pillars are great, including a chat with the previous landlord/property manager. I've had several tenants pay double rent, so they could provide proper notice and give themselves more time to move in.

I want you to be very cautious around any exceptions to this step. We've found many potential tenants who didn't provide proper notice. A lot of tenants don't know how much notice they're supposed to give.

We've had cases where we've made an exception, the tenant passed all the other screening criteria, but right before they signed the lease, they said, "Sorry, I cannot move right now."

Pillar 3 – Personal Reference

This step is important because if a potential tenant cannot pro-vide you with a name and number of a person who can vouch for them, that's likely a red flag moment. People generally associate with people who are similar to them. If the tenant provides you with a name and number of someone close to them, it means they're likely of similar mindset.

You can ask questions like the following:

How long have you known them?

Are they trustworthy?

Would you rent them an apartment, and why?

Are they clean?

How long have they worked at their current job?

Pillar 4 – Income Verification

Be careful with this one.

You cannot discriminate against someone based on the source of income; however, you can turn someone down if they cannot verify what they're making.

I also want to note that often, direct payment from some government organizations can be stopped at anytime at the request of the tenant. Just because someone claims you will get paid directly all the time may not be as good as it sounds.

When calling an employer, don't trust the phone number they give. Make sure you google the company name and search for other contact names and numbers. We have caught people giving us numbers of friends instead of their employer.

When you do call the employer, ask how long they've worked there, what the rate of pay is, and what kind of worker they are.

I do have to warn you, that where they work and the personality of the person answering the phone will determine how much information you get.

Oftentimes, you may get a contact in a large human resources department, and they won't provide any information. They may not even be willing to tell you if the person works there.

You can ask the potential tenant for a paystub, which can act as confirmation, or bank statements/cancelled checks, proving payment.

Summary:

Make sure you develop a proper screening process. Make sure the process is the same for all potential tenants.

Don't stray from the process. Realize that once the tenant is selected and a lease is signed, they're very difficult to get rid of if the relationship turns bad. Choose wisely.

How to Make the Perfect Rental Application

The rental application is one of the most important documents a property manager can have. There are lots of tenancy applications available online. We've tried various applications from one-pagers with limited information to two-page applications that have too much information.

We've found applications that we thought were perfect, then we would use them a few times and discover things we would like to change.

Shelly and I decided to make what we consider the perfect application. We built it in Word, so if you like it or want to change it for yourself, please feel free to email me fortnovagroup@gmail.com and I'll send you a copy.

We identified all the most important information and managed to put it all on a one-page document.

If you plan to make your own application or use someone else's, make sure it asks for all the information you need. If you plan to do a credit check, you'll need quite a bit of information.

Make sure every bit of information is necessary. Then you can tell your applicant to fill it out completely. Don't ask for information that's not absolutely required to process the application. In general, most people don't like filling out forms.

Here are the flaws we've found in many applications:

Application layout does not flow: If the information you're asking for doesn't flow, your applicant may not fill it all out. An example of information not flowing would be if the order were mixed up. We've seen applications that ask for the applicants basic info, then employment, then previous landlords. The problem happens when it asks for personal information, then a current address, then employment, then a previous address.

Application is too long: We've seen several two-page applications. This can cause information overload. In a lot of cases, some of the information isn't necessary. We've noticed when we're showing an apartment and the prospect asks for an application, if it's short, they will often fill it out on the spot. If it looks long, they may say something like, "I'll take it with me and get back to you." But they usually don't.

Application doesn't have the correct information required for a credit check: If you do credit checks through a tenant verification agency, it will ask you for things like the prospect's previous address. Also the basic credit check requirements are full name, date of birth, government ID number, and a signature line with a disclosure to let your prospect know that you'll be checking credit.

Application only asks for partial information: We've seen applications that might ask for the address but don't specify needing the postal code. Another example would be asking for employment information but not asking for the amount of monthly income.

Shelly and I decided to make what we consider the perfect application. You can download a free copy of it on our website at http://www.landlordbydesign.com/

Whatever your application process is, make sure you do credit checks and proper background checks on all your applicants.

How to Identify Red Flags When Screening Tenants

Proper tenant screening is likely the most important part of property management. Property managers and landlords not only have a responsibility to follow a screening process but they also have a duty.

When we show apartments and talk to potential tenants, we can often identify red flags.

Looking for red flags starts in the prescreening that we do before we show an apartment. It doesn't end until the application is either accepted or rejected. We need to ask lots of questions, just as your tenant will ask you a lot of questions to see what you're going to be like as a landlord/property manager.

What I mean by red flags are signs of an application challenge that may lead to turning down an application. We often see the red flags at the prescreening level. We often ask questions over email, but the potential tenant won't even respond. We've also had some potential tenants not follow through with their application when they find out we do credit checks.

Red Flag Number One:

Prospect doesn't want to provide government ID number so you can do a credit check – I remember asking a gentlemen for his government ID information on an application and he got very defensive, saying things like, "Rent isn't a loan. Why do you need to check our credit?" A person is **not required by law** to provide a government number to a landlord; however, it's a very important piece of information when doing a credit check. If you don't have it, you could get a negative report on a prospect, by having a mistaken identity. I have never had a problem getting this information from prospects who qualify to rent from us. I would consider it a red flag if they don't want to provide it.

Red Flag Number Two:

Employment reference phone number is wrong or fake – We always do an employment verification check. I'm aware that most organizations aren't very open with employee information. Here are a few tricks:

Always google the employer. Try to match up the phone numbers or people with the pictures/writing on the website. Does the company exist? Do they or the contact person they gave you work there?

Next, use the phone number from the website (the prospect may have given you a fake number). Call and ask for your prospect. (We've had employers say, "We do not know who that is.) When you do reach an employer who knows them, ask how long they've worked with the organization and how much they get paid (companies usually don't provide this information, unless the prospect asks them to.)

Make sure you have your prospect talk to the HR department, so they're expecting a call from you.

Another tip is to call and ask a random question. Shelly called an employment reference once and it appeared to be a friend of the prospect, who she caught off-guard, since she asked a random question "Do you have any water heaters in stock?" Use a question that relates to the business. She called another one and the person had only just started (they wrote down one year on their application).

Red Flag Number Three:

The tenant provides too much information – This next one contradicts what I'm always preaching: "gather information." We've had cases where the prospect gave us too much information. The great thing about people is that they love the sound of their own voice. We've had several cases when the prospect told us terrible stories about their current landlord and living conditions, how they had withheld rent from the current landlord, were recently bankrupt, just lost their job, were social and liked to party, weren't concerned about giving proper notice to the current landlord, were evicted, etc. I'm amazed at some of the things people will tell us. It's important to listen to your prospect; however, be careful.

Red Flag Number Four:

Not showing up – when you book an appointment for a viewing, we expect the prospects to show up. The reality is that only about half even show up at all. I wouldn't instantly disqualify a tenant for being a no-show; however, I would tread lightly. If they don't respect your time, how can you expect them to pay on time? Now, they might have had a traffic accident or something drastic. If that were the case, you may want to give them a second chance.

Red Flag Number Five:

Prospect will only provide vague information – They seem a bit uncertain when you ask simple questions like what's your current address? Where did you live before that? I'm not talking about a shy person; I'm talking about a person who doesn't seem to know where they've been living the past few years. We always like to contact two landlords. The current one may lie because they could be trying to get rid of them. Make sure to get a complete application. Explain to your prospect why you need the information you're asking for. Make them aware that having complete information will make the approval process quicker.

I'm sure there are other red flags when you're screening tenants. Sometimes, you need to use your gut. Professional tenants can be great storytellers. Have a process, and don't stray from it.

Do at least the basics:

Application form – with names, Government ID, employment, two past addresses, number of occupants, references, and signatures.

Do a credit check.

Call current employer.

Call all references.

Call current and previous landlord.

Get a copy of Government ID

Use your intuition.

If you do all of the above, you will limit your exposure to negative tenant experiences. I'll tell you the good news—most tenants are great. They pay the rent and look after their homes. I know when I was a tenant in the past, I never caused any trouble and always paid the rent on time.

Should You Negotiate Rent?

This is an interesting topic. We've been asked for reductions on rent for all types of reasons.

Our most common answer is "No, we don't negotiate on rent." We run a professional business, and we know the market; however, I figure since this topic has a lot of grey areas, I'll share some stories, and you can decide what the best strategy is for you and your business.

Story 1: Gut feeling turned into a long-term tenant – We had just finished a major renovation on a two-unit property. The units turned out better than expected and we figured they would command top-market rent. One unit we had occupied right away and then we placed an ad for the second unit. We had some viewings and even a couple of applicants who didn't work out. Then I showed it to a guy who had a great job and loved the location. He seemed to really like the apartment, but when I asked if he'd like an application, he said, "I would have to think about it." Oftentimes, that's not a good phrase to hear because if he truly thought it was great, he would want to fill out an application. My gut told me he was perfect for the place, so I asked him what his hesitation was. It turned out that it was a great place, except the price was just a bit higher than what he had budgeted, so he figured he'd continue his search. In this case, we had bought this property vacant, and didn't have any rental history, so I thought that maybe I was overpriced a bit for the market. I worked out a deal for $50 per month less. He filled out an application, it checked out great, and I had an awesome tenant for three years. In this case, I felt my asking price was a bit above market. That's not where I want to be. In my opinion, I would argue the sweet spot is just below market; then if you look after your properties and any tenant concerns, they'll stay longer. If you're over market, someone might agree to rent for a bit, but if they feel they're overpaying and similar places come on the market for less, they'll likely move. We all know the cost of a turnover can quickly eat up revenue. My point is that if you're asking the right price, you shouldn't have to negotiate.

Story 2: Reduced rent for service – We had a rental property that had a lawn that we would cut. I would personally go over and cut the lawn every couple of weeks. It wasn't a huge deal, but, as our business grew, it became more of a challenge. I decided I would ask one of the tenants on the property that if I provided the whipper snipper and lawn mower and they were willing to mow and trim the lawn, I would give them a $25 per month rent reduction. The tenant thought it was a great idea, and mowed the lawn for as long as they lived there. It was a win-win for both of us.

Story 3: Kijiji offer – We have an awesome classified ad site that we use for listing our properties for rent. It is very effective, but it does have one drawback. It's a free site, and you cannot control who uses it, or what they might say or email to you. I find it strange that people would make an offer on something they haven't seen and to people they've never met; however, it does happen. We don't respond to these types of offers. If someone were serious, they should be considering it's a home. They wouldn't just send a random offer. I'll give you an example: we might have a place advertised for $1,000 plus utilities, and someone will email and ask, "Would you take $800 utilities included?" or "I'll give you $900 including utilities" or something like that. We might be missing out by not taking these types of leads seriously, but I am willing to take the risk.

Story 4: Multiple unit discount – This has happened to us a few times where one person or family will want to rent more than one unit. We have given a price concession in these cases. I will caution you to not get too carried away. Reducing the revenue in a building should always be taken seriously. The margins are already very thin.

Story 5: The no reason discount – Sometimes, people ask for a discount for the sake of asking. It's important to not get offended. We've had some great tenants over the years who started out by asking for a rent reduction when they applied. They often back it up with a list of their great tenant qualities, but forget that the market determines the amount of rent, and since you only accept qualified applicants, all your tenants will exhibit similar qualities. I admit that I often ask for discounts or better prices when I'm shopping for just about anything. It doesn't mean I'm not willing to pay the asking price; I just figure it never hurts to ask. So it's understandable when someone asks for lower rent. We just say no.

Story 6: Retired/senior citizen all in pricing – We often find that when we rent to some seniors, they're concerned about the cost of utilities, since they're often on a fixed income. Seniors are often great tenants and stay for a long time. We'll usually work a deal with them.

CHAPTER 4 – PLACING YOUR SELECTED TENANT

"Excuses are the nails used to build a house of failure" —Don Wilder

I want this section to be more than just about offering a rental to a person or family. Tenant placement is too important to just make it a paragraph in this book. It needs to be broken out into a few different pieces.

We will start with offering the rental to your screened tenant. A lot of things can happen after that.

Offering the rental unit. Once you've qualified a tenant, it's important to reach out and offer the unit to them. Sometimes, when you call to offer the tenant the apartment, they've already selected another place, or they might flat out say, "No thanks." This can be disappointing, but don't take it personally. It's all part of the business. When you contact the selected tenant, congratulate them; make sure they know they're an important customer and you appreciate them. A tenant-landlord relationship needs to be a good business relationship for both parties.

Follow these two steps:

- If they accept the apartment, set up a time to sign a lease.
- If they decline the apartment, move along to the next screened applicant.

How to Provide Exceptional Customer Service

Customer service is a term we hear a lot. I often hear more stories of poor customer service rather than great customer service. If you're in any type of business, it's important to realize that an angry customer is much more vocal than a happy one.

When you're managing properties, it's really important to focus on great customer service. It can help with tenant retention, and job satisfaction for the property manager and owner.

Learning about customer service is critical for every property manager. The tenants who rent from you are an extremely important component to the rental business. They provide the revenue to the income property.

There are three main components to providing great customer service in the rental business:

- Communication
- Attitude
- Relationships

Communication:

Communication is extremely important to your success. The most important step in communication is listening.

Be ready to listen (get away from phones, papers on your desk, people walking around, or any other distractions).

Be an active listener (pay attention to both verbal and nonverbal language; observe the body language).

Active listening requires the listener to be engaged (make eye contact, ignore everything else, ask questions, make sure you understand).

When you're dealing with a tenant, you need to make them feel important. Maintaining eye contact can help keep you focused and shows them they have your full attention. Pay attention to body language. Is it opened or closed, friendly or aggressive?

You can also ask open-ended questions such as, "Can you tell me more about the situation?"

Show appreciation for their concern. You can say something like, "Thank you for bringing this to my attention?" If you don't know if a problem exists, you cannot solve it. It's better to know about a problem and have an opportunity to solve it, rather than not knowing until the tenant leaves.

It's also a great idea to take notes. That way, you can write down action items; it will ensure you have a full understanding of the problem.

When the tenant has finished talking, give them a summary of what they just told you. You can start this part of the conversation by saying, "Just to make sure I'm clear, can we review?" or something like that. When you've completed your summary, ask, "Is there anything else?" Make sure to address all the concerns. This is especially important if the tenant is angry. If you use the above technique, it will help you deal with a confrontational tenant.

Attitude:

Attitude is everything. If you dish out a great attitude, it will come back to you.

If you're involved in customer service, you should already have a great attitude. Having a positive attitude is the basis for excellent communication and customer service.

Make sure you pay attention to your attitude. We can all recall situations when a person with a poor attitude made a negative situation or experience even worse. Answer the following questions: Do you maintain eye contact when speaking to people? Do you greet tenants with your head up and a big smile (both on the phone and in person)? Do you take responsibility for your mistakes and apologize?

When you demonstrate a positive attitude, it's amazing how it will impact everyone you come in contact with. It may not solve your problems; however, if you have a difficult tenant situation, it can make it a lot easier to deal with. When you're dealing with an angry tenant, remember that the poor attitude they're exhibiting might be based on a poor experience in the past.

Make sure to view negative experiences as learning experiences. Look for the good in everyone. Don't take the situation personally.

Relationships:

It's important to form a great relationship with your tenants. You don't want to be super nice before they move in, and then as soon as they move in, you don't bother with them anymore.

It is important to realize that great tenants have choices. The cost of turnover in our rental business averages $1,000 in paint and decorating, and if we hire a placement specialist, it can cost an additional half to full month's rent.

We strive to avoid tenant turnover by providing exceptional service to our existing tenants. If you build strong relationships with your tenants, you'll have less tenant turnover and low-maintenance happy tenants.

In our experience, tenants want to do business with property managers who are actively involved, will fix problems quickly, and who genuinely care about the property and tenants.

Here are some tips on creating rapport:

Show interest in tenants: Ask lots of questions, which can lead to finding some common ground.

Be friendly: It always amazes me how a smile can reduce the level of tension in a difficult situation. You need to be a "heads up" person. Always greet your tenants with a smile and a hello. Make sure all your staff and contractors are "heads up" people as well. Make eye contact and, just like your mother told you, use your manners.

Be an active listener: Listening is a physical activity; take notes, watch body language, repeat back what you heard to make sure you understand.

Come to a resolution: I know what you're thinking; sometimes, you need to agree to disagree. That can be okay in some cases, but make sure you've done everything you can to resolve the issue. I have learned over the years, that there's no victory award for being right. In fact, in the rental business, it can cost you money, especially if the tenant moves out.

I hope these stories help.

It Is All in the Lease

The lease signing is another topic that I could write a book on. A properly written lease is critical. Most areas have a standard lease. You can usually attach rules, and as long as they're reasonable, most tenancy boards will recognize them. The type of lease you set up will depend on the tenancy rules in your area.

We start everyone on a six-month fixed-term lease. That's because if we do any other type of lease, the tenant has instant tenure and is allowed to stay as long as they're paying rent. That could end up being a challenge. You need to discuss the lease and go over it with your new tenant. In our area, the government requires you to attach the tenancy rules to the lease. The lease needs to be taken seriously and you need to make sure both you and the tenant have identical copies. I've seen a lot of really bad leases over the years. That includes leases for tenants in buildings I've purchased. Make sure you research all the leases available in your area and select the best type that works for you and your tenant. Some examples of leases are: month-to-month, annual, fixed-term, weekly, etc.

I broke down the process into the following points:

- Draw up the lease and make enough copies for each tenant and a file copy for yourself.
- For each copy of the lease, ensure that all areas that tenants and landlord have to sign and initial are highlighted ahead of time so nothing gets overlooked at time of lease signing. This is also done so that once the lease is initialed and signed, each tenant and you have identical copies of the lease.
- Set up a time and place to sign the lease with your tenant(s).
- Verify type of lease:
  - annual,
  - fixed-term,
  - weekly, or
  - monthly.
- Once the lease is signed, each tenant gets a copy of the lease.
- Each tenant also gets a copy of the "Residential Tenancies Act."
- Collect a damage deposit not exceeding one-half month's rent at time of lease signing.
- Determine day of the month that rent will be paid (monthly, weekly, etc.).

- Collect postdated checks for rent (if that's how your tenant is paying their rent).
- Set up a day/time for the move-in inspection.

The lease is the most important document that the landlord/property manager and the tenant have. It needs to be taken seriously. Shelly and I have often compared it to a marriage or a loan (please see the section on how to do a proper lease signing). There are several different types of leases, and it's extremely important to know which one you should use.

The following are questions and answers to help you decide which lease is best for you and your tenants.

What kind of lease terms are available in your province or state?

The kind of leases available in our area are fixed-term, weekly, month-to-month, and annual.

A fixed-term lease has a defined beginning and end. It can be 3 months, 6 months or 1 year. Notice doesn't have to be provided, and the tenant or landlord doesn't have to extend it any longer than the defined term. They do have the option to sign a new lease after the defined time. The tenure rules don't apply, since it's a specific term. We always start with a six-month fixed term and then if it is going well, we talk to the tenant at four months. That way, we can prepare to fill the vacancy if they're going to leave, or sign a new lease.

A weekly lease requires one week's notice by the tenant or notice by the landlord for specified reasons.

A month-to-month lease requires one month's notice by the tenant or notice by the landlord for specified reasons.

In an annual lease, the tenant needs to give 3 months' notice before the end of the lease, or it will be automatically renewed. The landlord can only give notice for specified reasons.

What are the tenant tenure rules in your province or state?

In Nova Scotia, the residential tenancy rules changed a couple of years ago. The biggest change was that as soon as a tenant moves in, they have tenure. The previous rule was that a tenant had to live in a place for five years before they had tenure. Please note that the tenure rule doesn't apply to fixed-term leases.

What does this mean for landlords in plain English?

The moment a tenant takes possession of a property, they have all the residential tenancy rights stacked in their favor. They still have to abide by the terms of the lease; however, you cannot remove them from the property unless they stop paying rent, violate the terms of the lease, you as the owner plan to move in (or have a relative move in), or you are doing a major renovation that makes the unit unliveable.

We've found the best lease to start any new relationship with is a fixed-term. We start with a six-month fixed-term, with an option to renew as long as everything is going well for both the tenant and the building owner. The six-month period gives both the tenant and us enough time to make sure it's going to be the right fit. If either party doesn't think it's the right fit, no other paperwork needs to be done. When the fixed term ends, the tenant can just walk away. If the relationship is working out well, then all that needs to happen is to sign a new lease. At the end of the six-month term, you can be a bit more flexible on how to proceed, you can also reach out to the tenant at the three or four months and give yourself a good amount of time to fill the vacancy. I will caution you that if you sign a month-to-month lease, realize that the tenants only need to provide one month's notice. That can put you in a serious time crunch to fill the vacancy.

What is your long-term plan for the property, and how long do you plan to lease the property?

When you're leasing a property, it's important to know your long-term or short-term plan. If you're planning a major renovation sometime in the next 2 years, then you may only want to do fixed-term leases. Fixed term leases will give you the specified time of when the property will be vacant.

How long does the tenant plan to live in the property?

When you're working out the details of the lease application with your potential tenant, it would be a good idea to ask how long they plan to live on the property. It might be easiest to write up a lease that works with the tenant's timeline. For example, if they're moving to a particular city in one year, it might be a good plan to write a one-year fixed-term or do two 6-month fixed-terms.

I hope this section gives you some insight into the types of leases that may be available in your area.

Make sure you use the best type of lease for you and your tenant (it's a customer service business), know the rules, make sure to screen, and build your portfolio with loyal, long-term tenants who always pay the rent on time and enjoy leasing from you.

How to Do a Proper Lease Signing

The lease is the agreement between the landlord and the tenant. It's a legally binding contract.

I have a friend in the industry who gave me some advice. Think of the lease agreement as a loan. If the rent is $1,000 for a 12-month lease, think of it as a loan for $12,000. What kind of paperwork and security would you want for a $12,000 loan?

The lease needs to be taken seriously; however, whenever we consult on tenant issues, the first thing I ask for is the current lease. What I find amazing is how many people don't have a current lease, or it's unsigned or incorrectly filled out.

I've also seen some poorly written custom leases. In our area, you're able to write your own lease; however, if you write into your lease items that aren't covered under residential tenancy guidelines, then those items will not be considered at a tenancy hearing.

For example, in Nova Scotia, you can only collect a damage deposit of no more than the equivalent of one-half month's rent. You can write in a custom lease, one full month's rent damage deposit required; however, if the tenant complains, you'll have to give half of the money back.

The lease should only be signed when all of the tenant screening is completed.

The lease should be signed in person (whenever possible).

Here's our lease signing process (based on Nova Scotia guidelines; other provinces and states may vary).

They have a standard lease form you can fill out on the website.

Make sure to fill out one copy for you and one copy for each person who will be signing the lease.

Then, highlight the areas you want the tenant(s) to sign and initial. We get them to initial a few areas, such as the tenant responsibilities section, amount of rent and when it's due, what's included in the rent, and acknowledgement that they received a copy of the lease and a copy of the residential tenancy guide.

Never assume anything. Communication at the lease signing is crucial. Go over the lease with your tenant (customer) line by line.

We've had questions about things that we think are common sense. Don't assume.

For example, when is the rent due? We always assume it's due on the first of the month, but if someone is signing their first lease, they might not know (we've been asked this question).

I have a friend who's in the student housing business; he rents rooms "all-inclusive." One Saturday night, he had a call from one of his tenants to ask for more toilet paper. When he explained that he doesn't provide toilet paper, his tenant responded by saying," I thought I was renting an all-inclusive room." The moral of this story is to be clear when it comes to what is and is not included in the lease.

Another important section is the notice to quit.

You need to be clear about when the lease is going to end, or what the options are to end it.

We start each tenancy with a six-month fixed-term lease. The fixed-term lease has a specific end. You don't have to renew the lease. If either party wants to part ways at the end of six months, we can do that. It's important to note, that if you do nothing but keep collecting rent after six months, it becomes a month-to-month lease, and the tenant will have tenure.

When you sign a lease in many places, you need to provide a copy of the residential tenancy guide. In Nova Scotia, if you don't provide one within 10 days of the lease signing, your new tenant can void the lease and walk away. We always provide a copy at the time of lease signing.

Collecting the damage deposit – We never consider an apartment rented until we have a signed lease with the damage deposit in hand. If it's close to the time the tenant is moving in, make sure to get cash or an email money transfer for the damage deposit. We've not had any damage deposit checks bounce, but have heard of it happening.

I would like to conclude by saying, make sure you take having a properly signed lease seriously. It's critical in having a great tenant/landlord relationship.

CHAPTER 5 - NEW TENANT'S MOVE-IN

"Customer service is not a department; it is an attitude" —M. Anderson

New Tenant Move In Checklist

You did it. The tenant moved in, the final step to becoming a landlord. Congratulations! You're now a landlord. But wait; you still have work to do to get your tenant settled. I also want to give you a bit of warning that, oftentimes, shortly after a new tenant moves in, you will often receive calls for deficiencies. That can happen for a few reasons. One might be that they're afraid if they don't point it out right away, they may be held responsible when they move out. Also, they might want to test your response time and see if you're going to be a good property manager/landlord. The other thing we've experienced is appliances breaking or other maintenance issues. It's all part of the business. That's why, once you get a good tenant, you need to provide exceptional customer service and keep them for a long time. Complete the following checklist to make sure you and your tenant have a great start:

- Complete the move-in inspection report before the tenant shows up.
- Meet the tenant at the apartment.
- Walk through the apartment with the inspection form and make notes where necessary.
- Collect first month's rent.
- Give the tenant keys.
- Confirm that your tenants:
    - know where to park
    - know where to put garbage and what day is garbage day
    - know where to put recyclables
    - know where to put compost
    - Know what they're responsible for such as snow removal, lawn care, keeping the apartment clean, etc.

    ○ know how to contact you
- I like to have a small "housewarming" gift and card at apartment at the time of move-in such as:
  - Flowers
  - Gift card for a restaurant in the neighborhood
  - Bottle of Wine

Move-In/Move-Out Inspection Form

All property managers and landlords should use a move-in/move-out inspection report. It is another piece of the landlord and tenant communication puzzle. In Nova Scotia and several other provinces and states, you can get a form to use online. The forms are free and, if used, will be favored by the residential tenancy board. Go to our website where you can get a free move-in/move-out inspection form www.landlordbydesign.com.

When we started buying buildings, we would take time to meet with each tenant to sign a new lease, and ask about any concerns. I have to admit that, even though we were diligent about the lease signings and doing repairs and maintenance work to make our tenants happy, we were a bit slack on filling out a report.

We were also a bit slack when we rented to new tenants. We would always do a move-in walkthrough and make notes on the back of the lease, but we didn't always fill out a form.

We're not the type of people who like to hold back damage deposits. We always like to pay it back in full when tenants leave.

This method of inspection put us in a bit of a poor position when it came time for those tenants to move out. If there was any damage that we suspected was done by the tenant, we couldn't be certain. We also weren't the best at setting our cleaning expectation.

I can remember doing a move out inspection with a tenant and she was so proud to show me around after she had spent the day cleaning. Let's just say I spent three hours recleaning the bathroom, stove, top of the fridge, etc., and, yes, I gave her back her damage deposit in full.

We learned from this experience that the move-in/move-out inspection report needs to be filled out for all tenants. It's not all about the form or creating paperwork. It's a great time to have open communication between the landlord/property manager and tenant to set expectations.

My idea of a clean apartment could be different from someone else's. The stage needs to be set. When a friend was moving out of a high-end apartment, the property manager tried to withhold his damage deposit because she found a couple of fingerprints on the windows and on the stainless steel fridge. This is an example of something that could've been dealt with during a move-in inspection.

I also found when I didn't do a proper form, I would always find myself being a bit of a soft touch during the move-out, especially if the tenant was a really great tenant, and they were moving on to buy a house or leave town. I know how important the damage deposit cash can be to a tenant, but I also know how important my time and money are.

If you do a slack move-in or move-out inspection, it will cost you time, money, or both.

Here is our current process:

When a tenant moves in, we go through the inspection form with them. We carefully note any damage or unclean areas. We take our time and explain/show how clean each room needs to be. It's important to show the new tenant how clean you expect the fridge, stove, and bathtub to be when they move out. We also note any work we're going to carry out after the move-in.

We have the tenant sign and date the form.

When we have a tenant move out, the form we use has a move-in and move-out section on it. We do a final walkthrough and discuss any damage that appears to be outside general wear and tear. We can refer to the notes on the move-in side of the form.

We discuss the damage deposit at that time. If everything looks good and the tenant is fully moved out at this point, we give them the damage deposit on the spot. If something else needs to be done before the damage deposit is released, or they're not fully moved out, we hold the deposit and tell the tenant exactly how much will be deducted if the problem isn't solved.

We have discovered that having a properly filled out form ensures a cleaner and more ready apartment. It also avoids awkward conversations with tenants who think you're withholding part or all of the damage deposit as a cash grab.

Should You Buy Your Tenants a Move-In Gift?

One thing we realize in the apartment business is that there's a lot of competition. We also realize that great tenants have choices. When a great tenant moves into one of our properties, we feel very fortunate.

The next stage to property manager/tenant relations is retention. Tenant turnover costs a lot of money (painting, repairs, leasing fee, etc.). Shelly and I came up with a plan to set the stage on move-in day for a great long-term relationship.

We like to show our appreciation for our new tenants with a move-in gift, and a welcome-to-your-new-home card. It's a small thing but has worked really well for us to set the stage for a great relationship. The new tenants really appreciate, well, being appreciated.

We buy a card, and then the gifts we buy are either consumable or perishable. Some gift examples are flowers, wine, craft beer, and movie or restaurant gift cards. The cost is usually about $25. We believe it's money well spent.

I'm not going to tell you that just because you buy a move-in gift for your tenants, they're going to stay forever; however, it does set the stage for the kind of customer service you're going to provide.

That's really important, since we often get compliments on our management style from the tenants. We enjoy the positive feedback, and your tenants will get peace of mind, knowing they made the right choice on where to live.

CHAPTER 6 - EVICTIONS

"In the middle of every difficulty comes opportunity" —Albert Einstein

This is an important topic for all landlords. I'm going to start with a few of my own thoughts; you don't have to agree with them. I'll start by saying that many evictions can be avoided with proper tenant screening. I'm not going to blame all evictions on poor screening. I would be a hypocrite if I were to say I've never experienced a bad tenant.

Another way evictions can be avoided is by being a bit flexible with the tenant. The object is to collect the rent on the first of every month from all tenants. I get it. Sometimes, property managers and landlords get very defensive when the rent doesn't get paid.

I also want to make it clear, that it's a good idea to start the eviction process on time and keep good records.

You can always stop the process at any time. Most tenancy boards would rather you resolve the issue with the tenant before a hearing.

As landlords/property managers, we also have to believe in the system. It may often seem unfair, but the system is there to protect everyone.

It's important to take a step back and look at it from a big-picture point of view. Ask yourself and the tenant questions like the following:

- Is this the first time the rent is late?
- Have circumstances changed in the tenant's life to make them late?
- If circumstances have changed, are they long- or short-term changes?
- Is there a co-signer on the lease to contact?
- Does the tenant have family who may pay the rent for them?

- What are the odds of them paying the rent from a gut-feeling perspective?

Try to take the emotion out (easier said than done) and think about how you can collect.

I want to share a story with you that happened a few years back. I had screened a couple and they rented a two-bedroom house from us. The first couple of months they paid on time, and then they were late in month number three. They didn't pay for the next two months, and we hounded them. They would just tell us not to worry; it will be the next day. Then the next day came and we would get stories of them having trouble getting the cash into the country. Then one day, they paid three months all at once with a money order. It was great that they were current, but it meant no more rent. It went back into arrears again. This time, we filed an eviction notice and set up a tenancy hearing, which, unfortunately, was two months away. The day before the hearing, they paid in full again. I thought it was really strange. We tried to make a deal, in which they could pay once every three months. They said don't worry, everything is sorted out. They will pay on time. That, unfortunately, was lip service. They went back into arrears, and we filed an eviction notice as soon as we were able to. Then, right before the eviction hearing at the tenancy board, they said they were going to move out, but wanted to stay two more months. We agreed, provided they paid all their arrears and paid in advance for the final two months. The amazing end of this story is that they paid, left on time, and left the place clean.

My point to sharing this strange story is that I really had to put emotion aside and strictly think about how I was going to collect the cash. I will admit I had a few nights where I went to bed angry and thought about a few not so nice ways to evict my tenant. I still don't know why they weren't honest about when they could pay.

Let's take a look at why someone might be facing eviction. We need to remember this is a business and, most importantly, it is a people business. What that means to all of us who rent just one unit or several, it's assumed that we knew what we were getting into, and, as business owners, are educated in the business we're involved in. If a restaurant gets shut down due to poor food handling in the kitchen, the government doesn't have any problem because the restaurant owner is assumed to know what's expected of them. It's on the restaurant owner to figure out how to properly handle food.

If I hear of a restaurant closing due to poor conditions, I say that's great news. The public and government put consumer safety (or perceived safety) before the consideration of the family and personal interests of the owner.

The reason I'm telling you this is to paint a picture of how landlords are often perceived by government agencies and the public.

You're assumed to know how to be a landlord. In most areas, the land lording business isn't very regulated. Basically, you can have zero experience or education and start renting a property. The property management business is also not very regulated, so even if you hire a property manager, you need to screen and manage them.

If you show up at a tenancy hearing or a small claims court, and you don't have proper documentation, seem scattered and unprepared, the presiding judge or panel will almost always side with the tenant, even if they come unprepared.

The expectation of the landlord/property manager to be prepared is much higher, and, in my opinion, it should be.

Why Do Evictions Happen?

Here are a few reasons and an example of a positive resolution:

The tenant loses their job and falls behind on their rent payments.

Talk to the tenant. Depending on the line of work they're in, it might be relatively easy for them to get another job. If they do get a job right away, then make a deal and add $50 per month to the rent until the arrears are caught up.

A couple break up; one leaves and the one left behind cannot pay the rent

Talk to that person. Perhaps they plan on getting a roommate. If it is a case where they're truly not going to be able to pay, see if you can place them in a cheaper unit, or make a deal where if they leave the place in 30 days spotless, you'll apply the security deposit to the arrears and write off the rest.

Criminal behavior, which is causing danger to other tenants in the building

Many communities have some kind of safe community's law. If there's violence, death threats, or other bad behavior, there will be a form of super-fast eviction. You may need to get a local government official and police to help.

A tenant gets sick, cannot work, and, therefore, cannot pay

This is always tough because nobody wants to evict a sick person. Unfortunately, you're running a business. It could be they're only behind because they're waiting on some sort of disability insurance. However, if they're uninsured and have no way to pay, I would suggest giving them 30 days to move out with no extra charges or problems, as long as they leave it clean.

Tenant starts drinking, doing drugs, or gambling

We've met people over the years who may have gone through a rehabilitation program to stop drinking or using drugs. Sometimes, these programs work, and sometimes, a person who was a great tenant for a long time could suddenly become a candidate for eviction. For a variety of reasons, a certain amount of the population will start or continue to partake in activities that turn them from being a great tenant to a bad one.

Domestic violence, which is causing safety concerns for the other tenants

This is another tough situation to be in. You may want to reach out to a domestic violence community group. However, if the victim doesn't want help, it can be tough. The reality is that it's unfair to the other people in the building to have to live in fear also. You may need to get police involved. You'll have to file the eviction based on the tenants being a safety risk to the other tenants.

They're a "professional tenant," someone who lies and enjoys finding and scamming unsuspecting landlords/property managers

If you have one of these, they're tough to get rid of. They generally prey on small, independent landlords who usually do sloppy screening, and don't properly fill out leases. They usually know all the rules, and even when you get a tenancy hearing, they'll find a way to delay it at the last minute. They're experts at playing the system. What you need to do, if you have one, is try to talk reason. You may have to bite your tongue and pay them to leave. It will be cheaper in the long run. You could say something like, "I'll erase the arrears and give you back your security deposit if you leave the place clean and move-in ready." The other approach may be to follow the eviction process to the letter. Try to limit communication and just get prepared and use the tenancy system to your benefit. Be patient; realize that this may take four months, but it could be a great lesson in tenant screening.

A landlord may evict to move into the property

This is perfectly legal in most areas. You will be required to give notice based on the rules of a particular area. Just make sure you're actually going to move into the property. Don't lie just to get rid of a tenant.

A landlord may purchase a property and want to do extensive renovations, so the tenant needs to leave

With the proper amount of notice, depending on an area, you can evict on the basis of renovations if the unit is not going to be habitable while undergoing the renovations. It could be you're going to gut and rebuild the bathroom or kitchen. In most areas, you don't have to rent back the unit to the same tenant for the same price after the renovation. It can be a way of getting rid of undesirable tenants in a building you're going to do a big renovation on. I've heard of this coming under scrutiny in several areas. So, be prepared to produce details and receipts for your renovations.

A landlord buys a property and wants to get rid of current undesirable tenants

When a landlord buys a building, especially if the plan is to fix it up and increase rents, time can be money. I've discovered that, oftentimes, even undesirable tenants will leave if you pay them. We took over a property that had a really dirty family living in one of the units. They were there a long time and always paid the rent. The problem was they were paying way below market rent, and, based on their heavy drinking party lifestyle, they weren't a good fit for the property. When we took over the building, we made a deal. We agreed to pay $1,000 plus give back their security deposit if they left the place clean and empty. I was concerned right up until the day of the final walkthrough. They took everything; it was amazing. No garbage bags, food, or furniture were left behind. I was more than happy to hand over the $1,000 and deposit so I could get started on the renovation right away. If we had not made a deal, the tenant may have left a dirty apartment and a bunch of junk behind, which would have cost more. Don't be afraid to pay some cash. Give people what they want, and they'll help you.

I want to point out that how you go about solving any of the above problems; the answers are different, depending on the area you're in. If you're buying properties close to borders, make sure you know the rules in the specific area you're buying in. One state or province may have rules that make a huge difference. Make sure you're fair and ethical.

Some places are landlord friendly and some are tenant friendly. There are specific guidelines and rules in every area.

Abandonment – AKA the Midnight Move

What if your tenant just leaves with no notice, no phone call, just missing? This has happened. Fortunately, it doesn't happen very often, but it can happen. If I had to compare it to the pain in the ass of a regular eviction process, I would argue it's better.

I'm going to share one story with you. It was winter and we have snow in our area, so it can be easy to tell if a place isn't being lived in. The tenant in this case always paid rent on time. They had lived in the property for close to one year and were on a month-to-month lease, so we had no reason to believe when they were late one month on rent that they were planning to disappear. If they were going to leave, they only had to give one months' notice.

I was doing a weekly drive-by and noticed it seemed sort of vacant. The tenant didn't have a car, so I figured maybe they just didn't bother shovelling the driveway, and it looked like there were foot prints leading up to the house.

I drove by the next week and the house still looked vacant, so I figured it was time to investigate. I have a property manager who collects the rent at this property, so I asked him to check it out.

He had already been trying to track down the tenant for payment, and wasn't able to reach him. When he went to the property, my suspicions were confirmed. The tenant had moved out, stole the washing machine, and left a bunch of garbage in the house.

The tenant didn't leave anything of value, so it was just a matter of getting our painter and cleaner onsite to fix it up and get it ready for the next tenants.

As soon as I got confirmation of the abandonment, I immediately placed an ad. We got immediate activity on the ad, so we focussed our efforts on getting a new tenant.

We didn't bother tracking down the tenant who left because, in my experience, you can spend a lot of time and money to have a judgement placed on someone who's never going to have the resources to pay you. These people generally will live their whole life this way. I was surprised, if they were able to get a new place to live, that the new landlord didn't call me for a reference.

When we took him on as a tenant, he didn't have much rental history but had great references to vouch for him. Unfortunately, the circumstances in his life led him to make a poor decision.

I'm not sure if you can avoid this type of situation; however, I do have a few tips to help if you find yourself with a missing tenant.

First, it's important to do weekly or at least bi-weekly drive-bys. Look for signs of the place being vacant. This is especially important if it's winter and you live in an area that dips below zero. You want to make sure they haven't disconnected the power.

When you suspect they have left, you need to make several attempts to reach them, including posting a notice on the door.

If they don't contact you, post a notice of entry. We just need to provide 24 hours' notice of nonemergency entry in our area.

If it appears that the tenant is gone but it's fully furnished, contact the next of kin or emergency contact they put on the application You may have to contact the police for help, in case they are a missing person.

If they're missing and the rent is past due, it's likely they have abandoned the property. A problem can happen if they left a lot of belongings.

When I've talked to several landlords about this type of situation, quite often, they will sell, give away, or put the tenants stuff in the garbage. The interesting part is that this contradicts most tenancy rules.

In most areas, you're required to store the tenant's furniture for a designated period of time, to allow them to pay you in full to get their stuff back. I know most of you reading this are likely rolling your eyes, and you're right to do so.

It is very unlikely you will ever receive payment; however, make sure you're aware of local tenancy rules and laws. If you happen to get on the wrong side of the tenancy board, you may have to pay a tenant for the missing furniture. The tenant could get awarded a significant amount of money.

Some interesting eviction stories:

My Favorite Eviction

This story is about an eviction. It was the type of eviction that I had only read about in books. It was a few years back, so I can look back and laugh. When I was dealing with the eviction, I think I went into a sort of survival, get-it-done mode. I learned a lot from the experience. It was one of those situations that make you stronger. It allowed me to see the best in people and the worst in people.

Let me explain what happened. It started with a poor screening job by a property management company (that no longer works for us). They selected tenants who paid the rent on time; however, they loved to party. They also had friends who loved drugs, swords, guns, and fighting with the other tenants in the building.

It became a regular event to have police show up, which lead to phone calls to me personally (since my property manager tried to ignore the problem). I asked our property manager to evict the tenants. She served them with a five-day eviction based on violence, and safety issues with the other tenants.

I was concerned that the five days would come and go, and the tenants would still be living in the apartment. I went to the apartment on day number six. I had already asked some of the other tenants if they had left, and it appeared that they had.

I rounded up enough courage to enter the apartment. The condition of the apartment wasn't great. There were cigarette butts everywhere, the bathroom sink was ripped off the wall, most of the walls had holes in them, ceilings had sword cuts in them, and food, dishes, garbage, and broken furniture were all over the apartment.

I was standing in the middle of the living room, thinking it was the fifth of the month and how quickly I could get it ready to rent for the first of the next month (I don't like to lose revenue).

I sprung into action. I went home and grabbed my 4 X 8 utility trailer, pulled it up in the parking lot and started hauling furniture outside. I started to create a bit of a neighborhood buzz, and people started asking if they could have some of the furniture. I gave most of it away, plus it was garbage day, so we convinced the garbage collectors to take extra. Then I brought the rest to the recycling drop off. I was able to make a lot of people happy that day with some new furniture, plus everyone who lived in or near the building seemed glad the tenants were gone.

I had my superintendent of the building and a couple of neighbors help me with the furniture and junk removal. Then I called a fantastic handyman and our plumber. I think everyone felt bad for me, so they sprung into action. We had the place back together and ready to go within a week.

I was also able to find a new property manager; they posted an ad and had it rented for the first of the following month.

Here is what I learned:

Proper screening of property management companies is critical to your business.

When I hired this particular property management company I should have asked more questions about their tenant screening process.

Having a team that consists of contractors, plumbers, electrician, handymen, and painters is also critical, especially in a time of need.

Even though there are people who do bad things, they're balanced by people who do great things. Always be grateful.

When you're backed into a corner, you can accomplish great things, especially when you surround yourself with great people.

Although I don't want to have another eviction like this ever again, I feel like I earned a few landlord stripes. I also hope by writing this story, it will show the importance of tenant screening.

How Do You Evict a Tenant for Bad Behavior?

I'm proud to admit that this problem doesn't come up too often. I'll also admit that this problem has come up. We can screen tenants as well as we want; however, we cannot control who the tenants bring to our properties. I also get this question a lot, so I know it is a concern for many people. I'll start with what bad behavior or (good behavior) is. Here's the Nova Scotia definition:

Good Behavior – A landlord or tenant shall conduct himself in such a manner as not to interfere with the possessions or occupancy of the tenant or of the landlord and other tenants, respectively.

As you can see, this definition is open to interpretation. If you have a tenant who is exhibiting unacceptable or disruptive behavior, you will need to contact the residential tenancy office. A residential tenancy officer will determine if the behavior is not good.

The length of time that the tenant will have to move out will be decided on a case-by-case basis.

There's one level above the "good behavior" clause. That is eviction based on safety and security. If you have a tenant who poses a risk to the safety or security of you (the landlord) or other tenants, you can serve a five-day eviction. If the tenant refuses to leave, you'll need to file notice with residential tenancies and wait for a hearing.

In Nova Scotia, a tenant cannot be evicted for doing something illegal, as long as it doesn't pose a risk to safety or is disruptive to the other tenants.

You can still contact the police (they may take care of the problem for you).

We've had to use the lack of good behavior section twice and serve a 5-day eviction notice. In both cases, the tenants left. One left right on day number five; in the other case, we made a deal and gave them a couple of weeks.

The first time was my favorite eviction, which I wrote about in the last section.

The second time, it was a problem with a couple. This couple seemed normal when they applied and signed a lease. They both worked and didn't have a problem meeting rent obligations.

The particular building they moved into had a mix of children and older people. It could be described as a quiet family building.

It wasn't long after this couple moved in that the complaints against them began to come in. It started with minor problems, like smoking inside and some loud music. They committed to turning down the music and smoking outside only. The next complaints involved these tenant drinking heavily outside in the yard.

They had not lived in the building long before we realized we had problem tenants. We addressed the concerns, and, in the light of day, they were very convincing. Then one Saturday night, all hell broke loose. I'm not sure, and will likely never know the full truth, but to sum it up, it involved loud music, drinking, fighting (possible physical), and a call to 911. The police arrived to break it all up. I have a property manager who looks after this particular building. He interviewed all the tenants. The clear message was either these tenants left or they would leave. The tenant with the children felt unsafe for her family.

I had a meeting with my property manager, and we agreed that, based on the other tenants not feeling safe, serving a five-day notice to quit (based on safety and security) was the right thing to do.

The tenants disagreed with the five-day notice. We then filed a notice to the director of residential tenancy. We had a hearing date set, but due to the overloaded system we have in Nova Scotia, the hearing was scheduled for one month in advance.

Fortunately, the tenants paid the rent and behaved perfectly, hoping we would back down. We didn't, and one week before the hearing, they moved out.

We and the other tenants were happy to see them go.

One thing I've learned as a property manager is that there's a basic process for everything. Sometimes, it takes patience, but if you stay calm and believe in the system, things will work out.

Can You Evict Tenants When You Take Over A Building?

I often get this question by landlords who buy buildings with undesirable existing tenants or tenants paying below market rent. When a buyer purchases a building, oftentimes, they will ask for vacant possession at time of closing. If this is written into a purchase and sale agreement, it's important for the buyer and seller to understand the law.

In Nova Scotia and several other parts of Canada and the USA, there are laws to protect the tenants and the new landlords.

When a building is sold in Nova Scotia, the existing leases are automatically transferred to the new landlord. This means all conditions and notice to quit by either the tenant or landlord apply as if the building never changed hands.

Tenants have to give proper notice, based on their particular lease, if they plan to leave (this can be common after a change of ownership).

Landlords have to provide proper notice also (this applies to an increase in the rent as well).

If you purchase a property that has existing tenants and leases in place, you cannot evict your tenants. Everything stays the same.

You cannot raise the rent without proper notice. According to NS Guide, p. 13, section 11, a landlord shall not increase the rent to a tenant for the first 12 months. If the landlord wishes to increase the rent, the following timelines apply:

(a) A year-year lease, four months prior to the anniversary date.

(b) A month-month lease, four months prior to the anniversary date

(c) A week-to-week lease, eight weeks prior to the anniversary date

You can evict tenants for the following reasons:

The landlord needs the property for their own use or would like to do renovations that require the building to be vacant. You, as the new landlord, will have to apply for a hearing at the residential tenancy office and the tenancy officer will decide how long the tenant has until they have to be moved out.

If the property is seized by a bank or other financial institution that is foreclosing, the tenants have three months to leave.

I've also had clients work out deals with current tenants. It's important that you make sure the tenant that you want to leave understands all their rights and is interested in making a deal. They need to know what their options are.

Making a cash offer in return for early termination of a lease can be a great way to deal with undesirable tenants. If you're planning a large renovation, I think we all know time is money, so what you can do is make an offer for a quick move-out. You can create a win-win situation for you and your tenant.

Here's an example of an early termination offer: Agree to pay your tenant $1,000 plus return the damage deposit based on certain conditions. A main condition would be to have the place completely cleaned out. Also, a condition would be that they move out by a certain time, ideally 30 days.

Make sure you're fair (perhaps on the side of generous) when making a deal.

If you're planning a rental increase, make sure to be sensitive, ethical, and fair. This can be a difficult conversation, especially if someone is paying way below market rent. If you're planning a large increase, let your tenant know what to expect. Spread the increase out over a certain amount of time. Communication is crucial.

I want to note that the information in this chapter is based on the Nova Scotia residential tenancy act, make sure you refer to your local residential tenancy guide.

Always Collect All of the Rent, All of the Time

As an experienced landlord and property manager, I've learned that, as much as you try, you don't always collect all of the rent all of the time and on time.

When I first started out and only had a few units to look after, I was determined to get all the rent all of the time.

The story I'm going to share with you involves a tenant who came with a building we purchased.

One particular day I went to collect rent from this cash-paying client (something we would never do now). I knocked on the door and she wasn't home. I asked another tenant in the building to call me to let me know when she showed up, so I could come back right away and collect the rent.

The call from the other tenant came in, so I headed there immediately. The tenant had most of the rent, but was short $5. I told her, that I had a 100% collection rate and, based on principle, I would need the other $5.

She said she would see what she could do and to come back in an hour. I left and came back an hour later. Sure enough, she had the $5. It was in a sandwich bag and consisted of various dimes, pennies, quarters, loonies, pocket lint etc... The great part was that I had the rent paid in full, which maintained my track record.

The next month, I showed up to collect and was faced with a story of not being able to get to the bank on time. I asked which bank she dealt with and she described a location that would be a one-hour walk or a bus trip to get to. This particular tenant didn't have a car, so I suggested that I drive her to the bank.

She agreed and off we went. I wasn't sure if she was going to walk in the front door of the bank and walk out the back, so I decided to follow her in. I stood off to the side, which was okay, but then she embarrassed me a bit when she was at the teller.

Here I am standing off to the side of the bank line and she's at the teller. She turns in my direction and asks very loudly, "How much is the rent?" I felt like some sort of evil, greedy landlord. It seems kind of funny now.

The good news is that she had enough in the bank to pay me.

The next month when I went to collect the money, she had it all. I guess she got the message that it would be easier to pay all the rent on time, so that she wouldn't have to deal with me bugging her.

It's important to set the rent collection expectation. We usually run into problems when we take over a property where the previous landlord or property manager was slack at rent collection.

We have a motto of providing good homes to good people. The reality is that if everyone is paying rent on time, we can focus on property maintenance and repairs. This benefits everyone living in the property.

CHAPTER 7 - INSURANCE

"Yes, risk taking is inherently failure prone; otherwise, it would be called sure thing taking" —
Tim McMahon

Insurance is the largest continuous expense you will encounter when owning or running buildings. It's a product you have to buy but hope you never have to use. If you do have to make a claim, you want to make sure you have the correct coverage for the problem.

I have interviewed some landlords who have paid off buildings, and they don't have any insurance. I don't think that's a good idea. If you have a mortgage, your lender will require you to have insurance. Your lender will likely only require you to have broadform coverage, which is, basically, in case the building burns down, or someone has a slip and fall and sues you.

What most landlords and property managers don't know is that, in most areas, insurance isn't government regulated. There are no specific guidelines on how much coverage you need to have, or what risks you need to insure against.

You'll need to source a good insurance broker who is familiar with the risks you need to insure yourself from. The mistake we made when we started buying rental properties is that we used the agent who sold our regular homeowner's policy. The problem was that she wasn't familiar with the risks involved or coverage available for rental properties. I'll share that story later in the chapter.

Insuring your income property is a lot different than regular residential insurance. The buildings may look the same, but from a risk side (which is what insurance is all about), the insurance companies assume that a tenant will not care as much about a property as the owner would.

Personal risk tolerance both financially and emotionally will influence the type of coverage you purchase.

If you have a high-risk tolerance and you never worry, you may choose to buy the minimum coverage you require.

In our area, many homes are heated with oil that's stored in outside oil tanks. The problem is that because of the huge cost to cleaning up an oil spill, most insurance companies only offer little or no coverage for pollution caused by oil tank spills. If you want pollution coverage, you'll need to buy additional coverage. The additional coverage can be very expensive.

Sewer back-up coverage. It can cover a lot more than just the main sewer pipe backing up.

My insurance broker told me a story about how a client brought him a competitive quote that was $250 per year cheaper. What my broker noticed was that the quote only included $10,000 in sewer back-up coverage. My broker asked the client why he only chose to get minimal coverage for sewer back up. The answer was that the house had an unfinished basement. That sounds like a logical response and a reasonable explanation, however, what my experienced broker pointed out was that a toilet could back up on the second floor and leak down two floors. How much would that cost to clean up and repair? What this client didn't fully understand was that sewer back-up insurance actually covered much more than just the main sewer line backing up. The inexperienced broker he was dealing with didn't know.

This particular client went with my broker and the more expensive quote because it had way better coverage and he wondered what else the other broker didn't know if he didn't understand sewer back up coverage.

Rental income replacement can be another important coverage. If part of a property burns down and it cannot be tenant occupied for several months while it's being repaired, your lender will still want a mortgage payment every month. Rental income coverage will pay you the income you would have been getting, had you not had the problem.

Deductibles and your personal financial comfort. You can reduce your cost of insurance by increasing the deductible you will have to pay if you have a claim. The deductible is your portion of an insurance claim. I always think of insurance as something I would use if something really bad happens. I would be unlikely to make a small claim. An example would be the time I had 4 inches of water in a finished basement. I go with a higher deductible to save money on the overall premium. If a claim is $10,000 and your deductible is $2,500, then you need to pay $2,500 and the insurance company will give you a check for $7,500. If you make claims, your risk level will increase, which translates into higher premiums. I go with a $5,000 deductible. I figure if I make a claim, it will likely be a huge expensive one.

Communicate clearly with your broker what you want to insure. Insurance is all about risk. The premium is based on the amount of risk (likelihood of a claim). The lower the risk, the lower the premium.

It's important to never mislead an insurance company. If a property isn't going to be owner occupied, make sure the insurance company knows.

If you plan to rent a basement suite or rooms in your house, the insurance company needs to know. The insurer needs to be able to make an accurate risk assessment.

They want to know things like the number of residents, proximity to fire services, what kind of heating system, age of the roof, age of the oil tank, and whether there have been any plumbing or electrical upgrades.

If you're new to investing, such as you purchased a house with a rental suite and you're dealing with a broker who specializes in personal lines (regular house insurance), you should have your policy reviewed by a commercial agent.

The worst case with insurance is to have a major problem, such as a fire or death, and the insurance company tells you that you weren't covered for the "risk." An example would be if a person falls down the stairs and dies, the insurance company launches an investigation and finds out that instead of an owner-occupied single family home (which is what the policy states), it's actually a non-owner-occupied student housing residence. Then they deny the claim. That's not good for you or the victim's family.

When or if you have a big claim, you'll be glad that all your i's are dotted and t's are crossed.

Tenant insurance:

It is a good idea to make sure your tenants have insurance. They might not realize how inexpensive it is. They may also not know about it. Your tenants' possessions are only covered if they're personally insured. A lot of larger property management companies require proof of insurance when they sign a lease. Make sure to educate your tenants on why they should have it, or make it a requirement of the lease.

Property Manager Insurance:

Many insurance policies will cover you if you manage your own properties; however, they don't necessarily cover you to manage other properties. If you plan to start a property management company, make sure to talk to your broker about insurance that covers you if a property owner sues you. It can happen that you place a tenant who goes bad and causes a lot of damage, and the building owner blames you. The coverage is usually relatively inexpensive. It could be around $1,200 per year. If you're already a realtor or a home inspector, your current error and omission insurance may cover you.

Also, if you have a large commercial policy, your insurance company will likely cover you if you manage a few other units outside. You'll need to ask your insurance company and make your intentions clear.

If you plan to turn property management into a business, then you'll need to make sure you have proper property manager business insurance, and make sure your clients are properly insured.

Learning About Rental Property Insurance

When we consult with people about property management, one of the first items we ask about is insurance. When we started investing in real estate, we were very underinsured. We didn't realize until one night I was at a real estate meetup and the guest speaker was a commercial insurance broker. What he said that night scared me, educated me, and forced me to seek out the right broker who helped us. The broker, who was referred to me by another investor, was able to provide us with the right insurance for not very much more.

I'm going to tell you my story and what I've learned about rental property insurance. I want to point out that I'm not in the insurance industry, and anyone reading this may feel I'm over insured or still underinsured. I realize that some insurance coverage is based on opinion or risk aversion.

Here's our story:

We had a house, motorcycle, boat, and a couple of cars insured before we got into the rental property business. When we bought our first property and I needed confirmation of insurance for the lender, I called our regular broker (whom we had dealt with for years) and had the person who answered the phone insure our new duplex. I didn't know what I now know, and the insurance I bought fit the profile of what the lender was looking for, so I didn't question it.

I thought I was insured. We ended up buying another four properties all in a corporate name over the next twenty-four months. I had this same agent keep adding them to our file. I, my wife, and our partner had to sign all the mortgage documents, and the agent never talked about a commercial policy.

I was shocked the night I heard the guest speaker at the real estate meetup talk about the type of coverage available for rental properties, and what kind of coverage property owners should have.

I often find that our story is similar to other investors. I know different provinces, states, and countries have different insurance coverage available; however, when it comes to rental properties, they need to be insured as a business and not as a personal residence. I'm not going to talk about hurricane, tornado, flood, or earthquake insurance, but if they're risks in your area, it would be worth investigating coverage for those hazards.

Make sure to get a professional commercial insurance broker to review your policy and make recommendations.

Here are some of the coverages we lacked:

Rental income replacement – this will basically pay you the rent while your property is being repaired after you have a flood, fire, or a covered problem that makes the property uninhabitable.

Sewer back up insurance – this covers the repairs required if the sewer backs up, a toilet over flows, a sump pump stops working, or many other water related issues.

Market value of buildings – you need to figure out the cost to rebuild per square foot and make sure you have enough coverage to realistically rebuild your property if all or part of it burns up. In our area, most regular owner-occupied residential policies have guaranteed replacement coverage; however, commercial rental property policies don't have this coverage.

Oil tank leak coverage – commercial policies in our area don't cover oil tanks. You need to get additional insurance to cover damage caused by oil leaks. Regular owner-occupied residential policies in our area will usually cover damage caused by oil leaks.

Two million dollars in general liability insurance – we did have general liability insurance, but it was only for one million. The reality is that it doesn't cost much more to increase it to two million.

We did have a regular policy; it's just that when you go from a regular residential policy to a commercial policy, you get a lot of business-related coverages that you don't get from a regular residential policy.

If you want to manage properties that don't belong to you, you'll need to get error and omissions insurance just like a real estate agent, home inspector, or other professional, who could cause a financial burden for a client based on mistakes.

If you want to manage a couple of properties outside your portfolio, you can often get your general liability insurance extended to cover you. You'll need to check with your insurance provider, and if you're going to start a full-time property management company, you'll need to get a separate policy. You'll need both general liability and errors and omissions insurance.

If you invest in condominiums, you need to be aware of how insurance works. The condo corporation will have coverage to rebuild in the event of a fire; however, the insurance company will only rebuild to original specifications.

Here is an example of how this may affect you:

You buy a condo that was built in 1985. It came originally with a laminate kitchen countertop and plain melamine cabinets. It may currently have granite countertops and cherry wood cabinets. Unfortunately, if the condo building burns down, the condo corporation insurance is only required to replace the kitchen with what was originally in place. You need to get additional insurance to cover the upgrades, even if you purchased the condo after the upgrades were completed.

I hope this overview helps you get properly insured. The point I want to make is that if you own and/or manage residential real estate, you need to discuss your insurance requirements with an insurance broker who has experience in residential and commercial real estate.

CHAPTER 8 - INSPECTIONS, INSPECTIONS, AND MORE INSPECTIONS

"Quality is never an accident; it is always the result of high intention, sincere effort and skillful execution. It represents the wise choice of many alternatives" —Will A. Foster

Types of Inspections

When you own or manage rental properties, having a proper inspection process is critical to your success. This is an area that I learned the hard way about why they're important. The other key part of the inspection process is if you inspect or have something inspected, and a recommendation is made to fix it. Face the brutal facts. It's better to deal with a problem quickly and properly. Just face reality and act. You're not alone. It is all part of the business.

Here are some of the inspections that you will need to do:

Due diligence inspections – These are the inspections you do before you purchase the property.

Move-in inspection – this is done when a new tenant is moving in.

Weekly/frequent drive-by inspections – this is done either once per week or two weeks and involves driving by and viewing the exterior of the property.

Exterior and common area maintenance inspections – these should be done at least every 3 months.

Annual fire equipment inspections – this could be smoke detectors and fire extinguishers or fire alarms and panels, depending on the size of the property.

Interior unit maintenance inspections – these should be done a minimum of every six months. It is the inspection of the inside of each unit.

Move-out inspections – done when the tenant moves out.

Vacant unit inspections – done periodically when a unit is vacant for an extended period of time.

Fire marshall inspection – the local fire marshal is allowed to contact you at any time and request entry to your property. They will make sure your property is up to current fire code. The fire marshal will likely have special powers to allow them entry.

Government building Inspector – The local government building inspector can request entry to your property at any time. If you're doing a renovation and it is not to code or you don't have the correct permits to be doing the work, they can order you to stop working.

The due diligence inspection process begins before you acquire a property. We bring a team with us to our inspections. They may not all make it at the same time, but we bring in the same crew every time. Our team consists of a home inspector, general contractor, radon inspector, and a sewer pipe inspector (he makes a video). If we're looking at a building 6 units or greater, we also bring in an environmental engineer to do a phase one study. I also want to mention that if we noticed extensive electrical, plumbing, or roofing issues when we first viewed the property, we often bring in our electrician, plumber, or roofer on inspection day. It's important to surround yourself with a qualified team of experts. Don't be afraid to pay good money for the right people. That way, they'll always be ready to work for you.

When the inspections are complete, evaluate the data. Roofs always seem to be a bit of a grey area. Unless you have documented proof it was replaced in the past five years, I would set up a reserve fund or be ready to replace it at a moment's notice. What we've experienced is that the roof that we think will last another 5 years usually leaks at around 3 years. When the unexpected repairs come up, it can be very hard on your wallet. It can also be tough, if you have joint venture partners, to have to reach out and collect money.

When you're collecting data from your due diligence process, make sure you're realistic on how much the renovations may cost. You may also be able to get some of them covered by the seller. But that will depend on how your deal is structured. It's common to go over-budget on renovation projects, so make sure to factor in some extra cash to cover the unexpected. You need to be ready to walk away if the building needs too much work. In our area, there are a lot of old properties in good areas that need a ton of work. Quite often, a person or family will inherit the property but not be interested in becoming a landlord. A lot of times, these kinds of properties haven't had any work done to them in years. The challenge is making sure to get properties like this for the right price. We've found many of these sellers want top dollar for old beat-up properties.

Home inspection – This is an overall general inspection that can give you an overview on what you're buying. The home inspector will be able to make a list of any deficiencies; however, they cannot see inside walls, sewer pipes, or air quality. They can tell you about everything you can see and can usually point out code problems like knob and tube wiring, 60-amp electrical service, no insulation in the attic, windows that don't meet egress, roof construction problems, etc. Home inspectors are great for giving you a summary of what you're buying. They're not great for telling you how much repairs will cost. You'll need to get an estimate from a qualified contractor or trades person.

Don't be cheap when it comes to hiring a home inspector. I can remember the first home inspector we hired. We were young and not very experienced. We were also stubbornly cheap. We wanted to spend as little money as possible on due diligence. We also felt if our realtor was giving us referrals, then they were likely getting a kickback, so they might not be working in our best interest (perhaps we were a bit paranoid). We found a guy in the yellow pages who had a long list of credentials and was cheap. He was $50-100 cheaper than all the others we called. Well, the guy showed up late. He appeared to be in poor health with mobility issues, driving a rusty old van with no logo on it. He did the job. Now that I've worked with other home inspectors, I realize he did the minimum and talked a good game. He definitely had lots to say. My point is to hire a reputable home inspector. Now that we have the Internet, it's easier to find good home inspectors with good reviews. We also look at the cost of due diligence as the cost of doing business. We're not afraid to spend money on due diligence to investigate a property properly before we buy it.

This has saved us much more than the expense of hiring the right people to check out a property.

Sewer pipe inspector videographer – We always get the main sewer pipe inspected before we purchase a property. The way it's done is that a camera is fed into the main cleanout. This will generally be located in the lower part of the house. If it has been covered up by a ceramic tile, drywall, or flooring, you can remove a toilet and use that sewer pipe. The sewer pipe inspector can make a video of what the camera sees. The camera will show if the pipe is laid on the correct grade or other construction problems, such as incorrect joints, blockages, potential blockage, signs of roots, stuff that should not have been flushed down the toilet, and the material the pipe is made of.

Some examples of what the sewer pipe going from the house to the road could be made of are PCV (plastic), concrete, cast Iron, clay, and a material referred to as "no corrode" which, unfortunately, is a softer material that tree roots and rocks can break through.

A lot of sewer pipe problems begin with the installation, so it's not just about the age of the property.

We experienced two tree-root problems that resulted in sewer backups before we started having sewer pipes inspected as part of the due diligence. It can be quite expensive to dig up your yard and install a new sewer pipe. It's better to have an opportunity to work a repair into the deal before you buy. We're slow learners, so it took two times before we saw the value in spending a few hundred dollars on a pipe inspection.

The company we use just does inspections, but doesn't do the repairs; however, many plumbing companies also have video equipment.

Tree roots look for water, if a joint in a pipe becomes dislodged or cracked either during installation or if the ground shifts, the roots will get in the pipe and grow until the pipe is blocked. We've also discovered poor installations where the grade of the pipe is either too steep or off in some way. This can cause items like baby wipes, thick toilet paper, bacon fat, etc. to build up and cause a blockage.

If you find a problem, one solution can be a liner (inserted into the pipe), or a machine called a Roto-rooter. It can be quite effective, and most plumbers have several attachments. Unfortunately, this is usually a short-term fix, and the real solution is to dig up and replace the pipe.

In most areas, you will be responsible for the sewer pipe out to your property line. If the tree root is through the pipe past your property line, you can send the video to the local sewer/water officials, and they will have to fix it. We have also experienced when we apply to dig, the city will do their part or allow our excavation company to do the whole job right out to the road. This does not save any money, but it is good to have the whole pipe replaced at one time right from the house to the road.

Radon gas test – this is becoming more and more common, and could be mandatory in the near future.

Radon is a colorless, odorless, radioactive gas that's produced by the decay of radium in soil. The emissions are caused by outgassing of rock, brick, and soil.

It seeps through the ground into buildings and becomes an indoor air pollutant.

It can increase the risk of lung cancer. Many lung association offices sell radon home test kits. Although it is a common problem in many areas of the world, it doesn't get very much publicity.

The solution is basically a fan under the slab of the house that vents to the outside.

It doesn't cost a lot compared to the risk of lung cancer.

The cost of the initial real estate 48-hour test is reasonably priced. The radon gas inspector will place an electrical box on a tripod in the area that's at most risk, which would be a room in a low part of the building that might be occupied for more than 4 hours consecutively every day. A room such as a TV/rec room or basement bedroom. The test company we use only does the test. Another company does the remediation. That way, they avoid any possible conflict of interest.

We recently had a test done on a property we purchased that was in a low risk area. The test came back positive for radon, so we had to have a fan installed.

Water/well pump test – if you're buying a property that has water provided by a well, it's important to have the water tested. I would also recommend a UV light that will kill bacteria before the water enters the house. The other test for wells is called a pump test. What a plumber can do is hook up a pump and time how long it takes to pump all the water out of the well.

Septic tank test – If you're purchasing a property with a septic system, it's important to have an expert check it out. They can do a couple of tests. Also, the seller will usually pay to make sure it's cleaned out, before a new owner takes over. If you're buying an as-is house, you'll need to check it out yourself.

General contractor – We always bring our general contractor with us on inspection day. That way, they can prepare and take measurements for renovations if we decide to buy the property. It's important to have a good working relationship with a general contractor who will be willing to join you for the inspection. The general contractor will be able to handle minor electrical, plumbing, and, of course, all the bigger repair stuff. It's also good to sell them a bit on the project, to show you what your plans are. This is especially true if you're into renovating and repositioning really rough properties.

Furnace/HVAC inspection – Many furnace/HVAC companies are willing to take a look at your systems in the hopes of future business. They usually offer this service for free or at minimal cost. Replacing furnaces, heat pumps, oil tanks, air conditioners, and air exchangers can be very expensive. We always have them inspected before we purchase a property. We also like to have them look at any ductwork. It's important to have your ductwork clean and not blocked; however, it's often neglected.

Optional based on original observations – When we look at a property for the first time it's usually with our realtor. We bring a clipboard and start making a list. When we do our home inspection, we like to line up all the necessary tradespeople on the same day. That way, if we move forward with the purchase, we'll have estimates that we can factor into the numbers.

Electrician – If a house has 60-amp service (outlawed in our area), knob and tube wiring, two prong outlets, lack of GFI plugs, questionable wiring, or if we plan to add items like electrical baseboard heaters, a garage, or extra units, we will invite our electrical contractor to the property on inspection day.

Plumber – Some common plumbing issues we've noticed on a first walkthrough of a property are corroded copper fittings, leaky pipe joints, improperly installed sink drains, loose toilets, pipes close to or installed against outside walls, no insulated pipes in unheated areas, no shut-off valves on sink water lines, and different materials or wrong sized joints joined together. If we see several of these items, it is a red flag that the house may need a lot of plumbing work, so we will invite our plumber along on home inspection day. That way, he can give us an estimate to have the plumbing brought up to code.

Fire alarms and equipment – If you're buying a property with a fire panel, it will likely require a fire safety plan and have the right fire equipment. This can include certain fire extinguisher number and placement, a written fire escape plan posted in the panel, and self-closers on all entry doors to units and exterior. Also required may be a proper amount of smoke detectors, metal entry doors that swing out from inside of building, metal door on furnace room, and an electrical panel not in the same room as washers. Drop ceilings may not be allowed between units, windows may have to be a certain size to meet egress standards for escape. It's a good idea to have a fire service company do an inspection of all this before you purchase the property. You'll usually not have to deal with a fire marshal inspection unless your property has five or more units. Also, if you are buying a student property or some form of a rooming house, the local fire marshal will likely hold you to a higher standard of safety compared to a single family or property under 5 units. It's good to be aware of what fire equipment is on your property. We know from experience that it can be quite expensive if a fire marshal decides to visit and forces you to comply with current fire code.

Phase one environmental – The phase one environmental inspection can be done by an environmental engineer. It's usually not a bank requirement on smaller properties, but it's becoming more and more common, especially in areas that are being brought back to life. The phase one environmental is mostly a research study. What they look for is past evidence of environmental issues on the property. Some of the things they have discovered that have saved potential buyers money are underground oil tanks. These used to be quite common, and are perfectly fine until they leak. They can also find things like perhaps the lot the house you're buying was the site of a toxic waste dump many years before and the soil is contaminated. If environmental issues are discovered during a phase one, then a phase two will be required. This can be very expensive and usually involves digging and doing soil samples.

WETT (Wood Energy Technology Transfer) – this is an inspection you will need to have done on any wood-burning appliance, such as a fireplace, woodstove, or wood furnace. The people who are certified to do this can let you know if your wood burning device is safe to use, or what upgrades are required. Many home inspectors have this certification. It's a specific type of inspection, so if your home inspector is certified, they will likely want an extra fee over and above the inspection fee.

That sums up the majority of due diligence inspections on smaller properties, you may need additional inspections depending on your area.

Move-in Inspection - Once you own the property, you'll need to do a move-in inspection with your tenant. This will require a form. The form we use has a side-by-side move-in and move-out inspection. Doing the walkthrough of the property with your new tenant is when it's really important to set the stage on what your expectations are. The expectations will vary depending on the current condition of the unit and the area in which it's located. Make sure you note as many deficiencies as you can to avoid possible disputes later. It can also be a good idea to take some pictures or, if you want to really step up your game, take a video of the unit with the new tenant. You also need to reiterate your policy on painting, pets, and renovations.

Drive-by inspection - When the tenant is in the unit, don't expect them to call with deficiencies. There are some tenants who call all the time and some you never hear from. Even if you hear a lot from a particular tenant, don't count on them to share the important stuff with you. I recommend a weekly drive-by as a minimum. This is something you can do in your car. If the property you're managing has a live-in super, you may get away with once a month. When you do your drive-by, look for abnormal things. I've noticed things like siding falling off, shingles missing, windows open in the middle of winter (in units we were paying to heat). I also check for flags in windows instead of curtains, or that the place looks lived in. If someone does an unauthorized move out, it is better to know about it right away. If you manage or own properties, it is important to know as much as possible about them.

You need to get out of your car and walk around and inside the common areas of your property a minimum of every 3 months to make sure there are no maintenance issues. In the past, while I've been inspecting decks. I noticed a couple that needed attention. I would rather spend money reinforcing a deck, rather than have a person falling through a deck and getting hurt. I've also noticed things like loose facia board and siding.

Fire equipment inspections can be added with the other inspections; however, if you have a building with 6 units or more, you should get a professional company to do your annual inspections. They'll make sure your evacuation plan is current, plus all your fire equipment is working and you have the right amount of working fire extinguishers in the right places. If you're doing the inspections yourself, make sure to change the smoke detector batteries once per year, and make sure all the smoke detectors work properly. You can do this at the same time as one of your regular maintenance inspections.We often notice that tenants will remove either smoke detectors or the batteries. This is extra common in units where the tenants smoke. We've experienced that a lot of tenants consider smoke detectors to be a nuisance; they'll take them down, perhaps with good intentions of putting them back up, but they never do. If you're inspecting your own fire extinguishers, make sure they're fully charged. Make sure, at the very least, every kitchen has one. When you're doing your move-in inspection, it's important to point them out and go over the operation.

The interior inspection. This has been one of our challenges. I would not be telling the truth if I were to tell you we're 100% diligent when it comes to interior maintenance inspections. We're a lot better at it now than we used to be; however, let's face it, if you have a really great long-term tenant, do you really want to bother them? The answer is yes. If you have continuous routine inspections, it can be better for you and the tenant. The key to success in this area is to set the expectation when the tenant is signing the lease before they move in. If their intent is to start a grow op, they might walk away at the lease signing if they know that you do a maintenance inspection every 4, 6, or 12 months. If you set the expectation and give your tenant lots of notice, it could be a win-win for both tenants and landlords. The most common thing I've noticed on my routine inspections is dripping taps. If you're paying for the water and you have several dripping taps, it can add up. We have also noticed things packed tightly against furnaces, bathtubs that need to be re-caulked, smelling pet problems, smoke detectors removed, cupboard doors falling off, leaks around windows, and many other maintenance items. The best maintenance is preventative maintenance. If you're hiring a property manager, make sure to ask them how often they inspect the inside of units. I have a friend who owns a couple hundred units, and he now sets up documented quarterly inspections. He feels it is important, and it would have saved him money over the past few years if he'd had a plan in place.

The move-out inspection. I believe it's good practice to do a pre-move-out inspection. That way, you can set the stage for exactly what's expected. I can remember doing a move-out inspection in my early days. I had a student moving out at the end of the year. I contacted her to ask when she would be done and she said to come over right away to see how clean the place was. When I arrived, she was showing me around with pride. The problem was that her idea of clean and mine were two different things. She either was a good actor or really didn't know what the expectations were. I didn't have the heart to hurt her feelings, so I gave her back her damage deposit and then spent the next three hours cleaning. The other disadvantage I had with this tenant was that she already lived in the unit before I bought the building, so I couldn't say with certainty what the unit looked like before she moved in. From that day forward, I made sure to set the stage during my move-in inspection and my pre-move-out inspection. The pre-move-out inspection should be done a few weeks before moving day, so it gives the tenant time to do any work that needs to be done.

The vacant unit inspection. This can be really important, especially in the winter and if it's long term. If you have a vacant unit, you need to check on it on a regular basis. Even if it's only going to be vacant a few weeks, make sure to turn the water off. If it's attached to other units, then make sure to close the shutoff valves on all the toilets and sinks. When you check the vacant unit, make sure the windows are closed (unless you're airing out the unit), look for rodent droppings, and inspect for water damage. It's a good idea to put some blinds or curtains in the street-facing window. If it's winter in a cold climate, make sure to have some heat on. You should always have power going to the unit, so make sure to transfer it into your name when the tenant moves out. You'll also need to make sure all walkways leading to the vacant property are free of snow and make sure they're salted. The bottom line is that insurance companies hate vacant units, so make sure you're familiar with your providers expectations when it comes to vacancies.

Fire marshal inspections – I experienced my first unexpected visit from a fire marshal a few years back. Up until that point, I guess I had been lucky. I always thought we kept everything up to code, but apparently not. I'm not sure if it was a disgruntle tenant who complained or we were just randomly selected. The total cost to get fire marshal approval was about $16,000. Here's my story. The bulk of the cost came from the location of the power meters. The power meters were located in the laundry room of the building. When the building was built over 30 years previous, that was likely not a big deal. We had to relocate all the power meters, so they were a safe distance from water. That was a major project because we had to upgrade the whole electrical system to pass current electrical code standard. The other items included things such as the furnace room door had to be made of steel, the back entrance door had to be changed from an in-swing door to an out-swing, some of the apartment doors had broken or missing self-closers on the doors that needed to be replaced, and we had to add a few more fire extinguishers, and make sure our fire safety plan was up to date with a copy submitted to the local fire department. If you're in the process of due diligence on a larger building, it might be a good idea to take a proactive approach and see if the fire marshal will come check out the building you're interested in buying. It can be a very expensive visit, if you're not expecting it. I know a property owner who was ordered to change every apartment entry door because the material the doors were made of didn't meet current fire code. It's a good idea for you as a landlord to have an understanding of what's required for fire code.

Building inspector visit – When you're doing a renovation or building, a visit from the local building inspector can be very expensive. The job of the building inspector is to make sure the rules and regulations for building and renovations are followed. They make sure you have proper government approval to do what you're doing. If you don't have the correct permits, they will give you a "stop work order" It forces you to stop your project until you have the proper permits in place. They will also not give you an occupancy permit until your building is built to current code and standards.

When you hire tradespeople and general contractors, you need to communicate with them about who is getting the permits for the job. Don't assume they're going to get the permits.

If we're doing a large renovation now, we'll contact the local government building inspector before we start the job. That way, we can work with them on what exactly needs to be done for code. We have them take a walkthrough of the building before we start. We've had a great experience doing this, since most building inspectors have a huge case load, and they end up in conflict almost every day. When we approach them, they seem to appreciate the fact we want our building brought up to current building code.

We learned this lesson the hard way on a renovation several years back. We had the permits in place, but one afternoon toward the end of completion, we were paid a visit from the local government building inspector. He took a walkthrough the property and made a list. The list cost us an extra $7000 in required work on a project that was already over budget.

The building was a 4-plex with two units up and 2 down. The front upper unit only had one entrance, so we had to build another set of stairs on the side of the house that led to a window. Even though it was just for emergency, it had to be built to current code with concrete supports in the ground. It had to be a top-quality set of stairs.

The two lower units had a door between them. The door had to be replaced with a metal door or the space had to be filled in. We decided to fill in the space. The house used to be an inn, so it had an inactive fire alarm system with pull downs and fire bells. We had to remove all of them.

That basically covers all the main inspections you'll need to do if you own or manage properties. I want to end the chapter with a couple of maintenance stories.

Do Not Delay Important Maintenance

We pride ourselves on looking after our properties, and are huge believers in preventative maintenance; however, we recently made an error in judgment in waiting too long to replace a roof, and it led to a leak inside the house during a recent rainstorm.

It all began about one year ago when a piece of aluminum facia blew off the edge of the building. I had my general contractor re-attach it, and had him look at the roof surface.

He told me the wood under the aluminum facia was in poor condition, and the roof appeared to be close to the end of its life.

It was a flat-roofed building, so I figured I would get a couple of quotes on flat-roof replacement and the cost of changing it to a pitched roof.

I had my general contractor price up the supplies for turning it into a pitched roof. He suggested I contact a roofing specialist to get a quote on both a flat and a pitched roof.

I contacted a roofer and when they provided their flat-roof quote, it was cheaper than I expected, so I asked them to price up the cost to change it to a pitched roof.

That is where my problem began, over the next four months it became a game of telephone tag due to some staff turnover. The roofing company I deal with also does snow removal, so I figured I would wait until March, then really be persistent and get the quote.

I know the company did great work for extremely competitive prices, so I wanted to deal with them specifically.

The unfortunate part is that due to my lack of persistence, the roof started to leak.

The great news is that I contacted the company that I was getting to quote on the job, and they came over and did an emergency repair. I really appreciated their quick action and help.

Here is what I learned from the experience:

The company I was trying to get a quote from obviously care about their customers and were able to help me in an emergency, so I really appreciated the service.

It would have been better for me to have been more persistent with this company or moved onto another company to get the roof replaced.

I also realized that I was really fortunate because we were able to stop the leak before it did any significant damage to the interior of the house.

It also reinforced the importance of preventative maintenance. I should not have delayed the roof replacement, as long as I did.

And, of course, I learned that I got my full money's worth out of the old roof. We used it right to the end.

How to Manage a Winter Vacancy

Having a vacant apartment any time of year can be a challenge. When you live in a cold climate, a winter vacancy can be even more challenging. This past year, we had an apartment where the old tenant moved out and there was a 30-day delay until the new tenant moved in.

In the warmer months, you still need to check on and maintain your property on a regular basis; however, the following are some of the extra cold winter challenges:

Heat – you must remember to leave the heat on. You can get away with it turned down low; however, do **not** turn it off because you require heat to make sure your water pipes don't freeze (if any water remains in them after they are drained). Another reason to have your heat on is to reduce the amount of humidity in the air. The heat will keep the unit dry.

Water shut off valves turned off – This is a good thing to do all year round. Your toilets, sinks, and hot water tanks should have water shutoff valves. If they don't, and, for some reason, a toilet or tap starts to leak, you'll have a flood. Water in pipes and in the water heater will need to be drained, especially if the unit will be vacant for longer than a couple of weeks.

Shoveling and salting – It's very important to make sure the walkways and driveways are shoveled and salted. It will make the unit looked lived in, and lessen your risk of somebody having a slip and fall accident on your property.

More frequent checks – If you have a vacant property, you'll need to check on it a lot, even more in the winter. If something bad happens, the insurance company will ask how often you checked on the property. It's very important to take a quick walk through the property on a very regular basis (every day would be ideal). The main reason is that you can have equipment failure that can result in a lot of damage. Some examples would be a furnace breaking down, an electric baseboard radiator failure, or a hot water heater leaking.

Bad weather can strike at any moment in the winter, so it's really important to be ready. We cannot eliminate winter; however, by following the above steps, you can significantly reduce your risk of costly repairs due to a winter vacancy.

What to Look for When Inspecting a Rental Property

I was inspired to write this section by an incident that happened the other day. I had to gain access to an apartment to check a ventilation system. When I entered the unit, I noticed the smoke detector was missing from the living room, I then discovered that the smoke detector in the hall (which was hard wired) wasn't working. When you see problems, even if you're there for a different reason, it's important to take action. It's impossible to un-see something. What I did in this case, was go to a local building supply center to pick up a new smoke detector. I installed it and got in touch with the tenant about the missing smoke detector.

It's important to do a walkthrough at least once per year to look for maintenance items. We have some tenants who will call us for minor problems, other tenants who never contact us, and, of course, everyone in between. If you're in a unit between your annual checks (as I was the other day) it's important to take a quick glance around. Look for things like dripping taps, water heaters, and washing machines, check around windows and doors for signs of leaks, and just inspect the overall condition of the unit. We've been able to solve several maintenance issues just by looking around whenever we're in a unit.

Property management is a physical activity; you need to stay in-volved.

I'm not sure if I overdo it, but I do a weekly drive-by on all our lo-cal properties. I don't go inside them, but I take a look at the ex-terior for anything unusual.

Some of the things I've been able to find and take action on are as follows:

Loose siding flapping in the wind – I was able to reattach it be-fore it was damaged.

Paint peeling – It's amazing how easily you can increase curb appeal with a bit of paint. I've noticed paint peeling around win-dows and foundations, and rust spots on doors.

Facia board – after windstorms, I've lost a few pieces of facia. I've been able to replace them, and sometimes I've been able to find the piece that blew off. I once discovered that all the wood under the aluminum facia on a particular house was rotten, so I was able to address that problem.

Leaning oil tank – I once noticed an oil tank that was leaning due to the ground shifting under it, I was able to contact a tank in-staller and get it leveled.

Overgrown bushes – I've seen small trees and bushes start to take over the front of a house. That can easily be brought under control.

Garbage and recyclables placed at the curb on the correct day – I once had a by-law enforcement officer contact me to say I would get a fine if I didn't remove the recyclables from in front of one of our houses right away. I got in touch with the tenant and they had gone to their cottage for a couple of weeks, so they figured they would place the recyclables out a week early. I went by and picked up the bag in question.

I also do a yard walk about every four months. It's important to take a quick look at the back of the house. Here are some of the things I have found:

Check decks – I noticed a deck starting to pull away from a house, I immediately contacted my general contractor and had joist hangers and proper bolts to support the deck installed.

Items placed on oil lines – make sure to check oil tank lines; it's amazing what you might find piled on oil lines. I've seen, rakes, rocks, bikes, and garden hoses tangled in oil lines.

Excessive dog poop – We allow dogs at some properties based on strict guidelines. One thing we require is that the yard doesn't get full of dog poop. Also, we check to make sure dogs don't dig holes. Dogs can do a lot of damage to a yard.

Garbage stacked up – we've been able to correct the bad habit of tenants stacking garbage bags on back steps or decks.

Neglected lawns – Some of our lawns are mowed by lawn mowing companies and some are cut by the tenants. Either way, we don't want our lawns overgrown. I can remember doing a drive-by on a property and I noticed the grass was getting really long. When I went by on week number two, I called the company that was taking care of the lawn. They gave me an excuse about rain (that's a common excuse I've heard from smaller lawn care companies). The good new is that they came right away and mowed it, and I never had a problem after that.

I'll save the annual inspection list for another section. I just wanted to share my story on the importance of being an active property manager.

CHAPTER 9 - COMMON MAINTENANCE ISSUES AND HOW TO DEAL WITH THEM

"The difference in success or failure can be doing something nearly right or doing it exactly
right." —Anonymous

Water/Moisture/Mold/Mildew/Odors

I want to talk about water, moisture, mold, and mildew. If you have rental properties, you will encounter one or all of these. Water is not a friend of the landlord/property manager.

It's really important to learn about, because pretty much every climate has one or all of these issues, and as soon as you have properties, you'll realize you have them too.

These problems can often seem worse than they really are, depending on the reaction from your tenants. It is important to look for a positive lesson in every experience. Sometimes you may have to dig deep to find a way to reframe a situation, so you can see it in a positive light.

I've encountered all of the above, so I'm going to share my experience about each one:

Story 1 – Water and the sewer back up – I can remember the day as if it were yesterday. I was out for a walk on a rainy February Sunday morning. I was with my family, so I didn't answer a call from a tenant. I figured I'd just check the message. I would call back after my walk. Then the same tenant called again. I found this unusual because this was a tenant whom I never heard from. They always paid rent on time and never complained. I answered the phone and my tenant (in her laid-back way) said we were getting water in the basement and I should come take a look. She said she first noticed it a few hours before, but she didn't want to bug me. I went to the property which is a side-by-side duplex and was shocked to see approximately 4 inches of water with more coming in through a floor drain.

125

I immediately went to the other side of the duplex and realized it was also full of water. Both sides were finished with rec rooms, and things were floating around the rooms.

I got on the phone to my plumber; I fortunately had his cell number and asked him to help. He was at a hockey rink with his family and said he would call his on-call guy. I met the plumber onsite within an hour.

What had happened was that the sewer pipe got blocked somewhere under the front lawn, and, in this particular building, the roof water drained into the sewer pipe. It was pouring down rain, so the water was draining off the roof going into the sewer pipe, hitting the blockage and coming back up through the floor drain in the basement.

The plumber said we would need a big heavy electric snake and a pump with a fire hose to get the water out. He said it was a two-man job, so I volunteered. It took some work and, at some points along the way, I thought the snake was going to break. We finally got through the blockage. It appeared to be a tree root. I was so happy to hear water starting to drain out of the house.

I then called my insurance broker. He got in touch with my adjuster, who contacted a disaster restoration company.

By 6:00 p.m. that Sunday, we had the water out and big fans in place to dry it out. The restoration company cut out the drywall up to about four feet all around. The next day, I ordered a dumpster pod. It was quite a mess. I did get to learn how good my insurance company was in an emergency.

The insurance company covered the damage repairs, but they didn't cover the solution to the problem.

We changed the roof drain system, dug up the yard to replace the sewer pipe, and installed a sump pump on each side of the duplex. We also upgraded the new flooring to a waterproof flooring.

The other problem was that one tenant had insurance, and the other had cancelled his insurance a few months previous. The tenant with insurance got money to buy all new furniture and paid for half of the pod. The tenant without insurance had to salvage his furniture and buy some new stuff. That likely cost him more than what he saved by cancelling his insurance policy.

Story 2 – Moisture – I received a call from a tenant who complained about his windows dripping with condensation and the back of one of his dressers had mold on it. At first, I thought about the usual causes of moisture (which can be important to point out to your tenants) such as not using the bathroom fan when showering, or not turning on the heat. These two things can cause the moisture problems he was describing. I decided to send my general contractor to check it out. He confirmed that the unit had higher than normal humidity, and discovered a leak in a window. We replaced the window; however, since it was a basement unit, it still felt moist. We came up with a great solution. We installed a wall-mounted fixed dehumidifier that drained directly outside. They work almost as good as an air exchanger for a fraction of the price. They use very little electricity and are a lot quieter than a regular portable dehumidifier. There are several companies that make them. You can google Nu Air to see an example of one. There are different sizes, depending on square footage. I'll say one thing we've learned about moisture problems is that you always need to find the root of the problem. A dehumidifier is not a cover-up solution; however, it can make a huge impact on the climate of a basement suite, or if you're in a humid area.

Story 3 – Mold – This was definitely a learning experience for us. When we were first contacted by the tenants, we bought a dehumidifier. A couple of months went by and we were contacted again (the mold came back). It was in the back corner of one of the closets. We decided to have our general contractor look for a leak or source of moisture. When he looked around the unit, he couldn't find a source, so he decided to check out the attic. The roof is only a couple of years old and vented very well. What he discovered in the attic is that the vent for the bathroom fan had become detached. This can happen when the clips that hold the vent hose onto the fan shrink. The sheathing on the inside of the roof was black, and some flakes of mold fell down on the insulation. We had discovered a mold issue. I never dealt with a serious mold issue and neither had our general contractor. After I had a small nervous breakdown, I collected myself and made some calls to mold remediation companies. The companies I contacted had a solution. It wasn't cheap. It cost about $3,000 to get rid of the existing mold, and the recommended air exchanger we had installed cost another $2,000. The first part of the solution was an education on mold. When I talked to the environmental remediation company they made me feel a lot better. I also want to note that our tenants were very unemotional about the whole situation. We kept them in the loop and they could clearly see we were going to go over and above to find the best solution possible. Once we fixed the vent and installed the air exchanger, it changed the climate of the unit. The air exchanger also pulls moisture out of the air. It's quiet and doesn't use very much electricity.

Here are some of the things we learned about mold:

It can affect different people in different ways. It can be similar to how allergies affect people. Some people are allergic to things like peanut butter, and some people are not.

Mold spores are everywhere. In fact, high concentrations of mold spores are found in nature, and in products such as bark mulch. The spores are just waiting for the right conditions. The best conditions to grow mold are moisture, darkness, moderate to warm temperature, and stale air. If you want to avoid mold, you need to make sure you don't provide ideal conditions. Some things to educate your tenants about are to make sure closets aren't jammed full with a closed door. If there's a water leak, have them notify you as soon as possible. If the bathroom is equipped with a fan, they should make sure to use it.

There are other solutions. Some might not be as expensive as ours. The bottom line is that you hear stories about black mold, green mold, and other colors. No mold is good. If you have mold, then you've created conditions for the spores to activate. You need to find the source of the problem and solve it. The solution could be as simple as putting less stuff in a closet and leaving the door open. It could be a simple dehumidifier. In our case, the cause was resolved, but we wanted to ensure it never happened again, so we used an air exchanger as the solution. There have been some cases where mold can take over a building. It can get behind the drywall and grow for a long time before it is de-tected. These type of cases can become a big problem. I have seen some buildings condemned for mold.

Remediation might not be that serious. It could be as simple as a bleach cleanup. There are remediation and testing companies that can help you. The company we used was very helpful. They put my mind at ease with a bit of education. The media has made mold problems much worse than they are. The reality is that mold is quite common, and can be remediated quite easily. In our case, due to it being on the inside of the attic, it was a bit harder to remediate, and special chemicals applied by profes-sionals had to be used. The chemicals they used were not harm-ful to the environment.

In summary, my experience with both the remediation company and testing company were great. I've seen some documentaries of testing companies ripping people off, so I was a bit concerned when I called them in, but the companies in our area were great and provided a lot of education on the subject.

Story 4 Mildew – mildew is quite common in bathrooms and on the inside of older windows. It's similar to a mold issue; however, it may be due to an unavoidable moisture problem. Most mildew can be wiped away, or on the inside of old windows, you can wipe away the condensation before mildew forms. We do notice mildew on the inside of shower curtains, and usually for the price of a new shower curtain, it is easier to just replace them every now and again. Even mildew-resistant shower curtains, paint, and cleaners cannot solve the problem 100%. We've had com-plaints about mildew from various tenants over the years. To solve the problem, it's often just a case of some education. You need to tell your tenants to use the bathroom fan when they shower. They also need to clean the bathroom, including the shower curtain on a regular basis. We've cleaned the inside of window edges for tenants, and then showed them how to do a simple wipe down to avoid future problems.

What Is That Smell?

In the landlord and property management business, you will encounter many odd smells. Learning how to deal with them will be a critical part of your business. Different smells affect people in different ways. I have a real estate agent friend who cannot spend much time in a building with a lot of mold and must. I've also gagged while entering several properties.

I'm going to break down this section into common smells and how to identify them.

It's really important to identify where the smell is coming from. It could be one location, a few, or the entire unit.

Many smells are hard to identify and remove. We have completely scrubbed, cleaned, and left windows open in apartments, but they still smell.

If you mask the smell with an air freshener or Febreze-type product, it will likely reappear. You need to identify the source of the odor and come up with a solution.

The smell in a unit may still have to be dealt with, even if the source was removed. This is common in smoked-in units. You can clean up the cigarettes and remove the smoker, but the room will still smell like smoke.

Common Odors You May Encounter

Smoke – Cigarettes and marijuana (aka weed) are common smells when entering apartments or houses. The problem when someone lives and smokes in a unit for several years is that the walls can turn yellow and be covered with a thick, gooey substance—nicotine. The best way to treat the walls in a smokers unit is to scrub the walls then paint. You will need to replace or clean any curtains and blinds. If the unit has carpets, you might be able to save it with a carpet cleaner, a steam cleaning carpet cleaner works best. These can be rented from tool rental shops, and even some grocery stores still rent them, plus many cleaning companies do carpet cleaning for a reasonable price.

If the unit only has a mild smell of smoke, you may get away with painting over the dirty walls, and giving the unit a good cleaning. Marijuana has a sweet or skunk-type smell, and as long as the tenants have not been growing it in the unit, the smell can be removed similar to cigarette smoke.

Dead rodents – when I first walk into a place, sometimes, the smell of death hits my nose. If you smell a dead rodent, it's important to start looking for it. Unfortunately, this may require sometimes putting a hole in a wall. Before you put holes in the walls make sure to check under appliances, inside cupboards and closets, and above drop ceilings. They can be in spots up inside the back of stoves or on top of dishwashers. Once the corpse is removed and the affected area is cleaned, the smell will go away.

Cat urine – This is one of the worst smells you can have. It's very difficult to get rid of, and will absorb into floors, walls, and carpets, especially if the cat was "in heat." A lot of landlords and property managers don't allow cats for this reason. If the unit has a floating floor or carpet, you may have to replace it and paint the floor underneath to seal in the odor. If removal of the floor is not an option, you will need to use cleaners like bleach or ammonia. Cat boxes can cause a unit to smell; however, once removed, the smell will likely go away.

Dog – dogs are almost as bad as cats, especially if they go into "heat." Dog smell often gets into carpets. You may be able to get a lot of it out with a carpet cleaner. If a dog has rolled around on a carpet for several years, replacement may be the only option. Baking soda and a good cleaning can make the unit smell dog free.

Rotten food – This can make a unit smell really bad. It's usually easy to find. It could be left in an unplugged fridge, cupboard, in garbage bags, or just about anywhere. Food can be removed, and once the unit is cleaned, the smell will generally go away. If you have a vacant unit, make sure to leave the fridge and freezer clean and unplugged. Place an open box of baking soda in the fridge and freezer

Mold/Mildew – I have a nose for mold, I can smell if a place has a moisture issue. You will need to identify the cause and take action to solve the problem. It could be as simple as a cleanup and the installation of a portable dehumidifier. This is common in dark basements. Once the source of the problem is handled, the smell should go away.

Construction/paint – When we have completed extensive renovations of properties, they will often smell like paint, silicone, glue, wood. My opinion is that it makes a place smell new; however, that opinion is not shared with all potential tenants. You may need to use a cleaner like ammonia to get rid of the smell.

Bathrooms – Bathrooms are a common place to find foul odors. Toilets can smell bad, sometimes we've had to replace toilets, and, in some cases, the floor underneath them to get rid of a urine smell. The square footage of most bathrooms isn't that large, so it can be worth it to remove the toilet, vanity, and flooring and replace it all. It can be a great way to increase the value in your property for a reasonable price.

Sink drains – Sink drains can often be a source for bad odors. What you can do is remove the cap on the P-trap under the sink. It can be a bit messy, so make sure to have a bucket ready to catch the debris. It's amazing some of the things that I've found in drains. I've found jewelry, utensils, small toys, baby wipes, paper towels, hair, and smelly goo. I will warn you to wear gloves if you're going to remove the cap on the p-trap. Someone may have poured Drano or a similar acid drain cleaner in the drain in an attempt to clear the drain.

Unidentified odor – We've had cases when after taking over a property and all the belongings have been removed, it still smells bad. It could be because of a combination of various odors mixed together. Garbage that was removed may have leaked on the floor, or the smell of smoke could be lingering in the air. It could be everything mixed together. I have gagged walking into several units. Sometimes, it just takes a lot of cleaning and a fresh coat of paint and, in some cases, new flooring or the use of an ozone machine is required.

Smell and Odor Removing Solutions

Ozone machine, the ozone machine will break down the molecules, bacteria, and spores that cause the bad smells. Ozone ($O3$) is a reactive molecule that chemically reacts with particles that it comes in contact with in the air and on surfaces. I know that may sound really high tech; however, an ozone machine (even a good one) can be purchased on amazon for a range in price from around $100 to $400. It will depend on how much ozone you want to create. Most auto detail shops will have one, so to give you an idea on the size, it will be smaller than a toaster oven, and most are about the size of a loaf of bread. It can be easily transported. It's great to remove the smell in a room after the source of a bad smell has been removed or a leak has been fixed. The ozone machine will get the air back to normal. An ozone machine can change a smoked-in unit to a nonsmoking unit in a few hours.

The day I got sold on the ozone machine was when I got stumped trying to get the smell out of an apartment. We had re-done an abandoned building, and one unit had squatters living in it. When we cleaned it, we found everything from dead rats to rotten food. We came across mold on clothes, a disgusting bathroom, rat urine, cat urine, you name it, and this apartment had a terrible odor. Even after we renovated and replaced most of the floor, the appliances, fixtures, painted top to bottom, etc., it still smelled bad. We tried Febreze, every known cleaner, bleach, and on and on. I would think the smell was gone, but two days later, it would be back. We had to come up with a solution and fast. I called a property manager of a company that specialized in renovating C buildings, so I figured she would have the answer. The first thing she asked was if I had an ozone machine. I said no, but I had access to one from an auto detail shop. I put the machine in the unit and left it for a couple of days. When I returned, the air was stale, but the smell was gone. I opened the windows to air the unit out and, as they say, the rest is history. A couple of weeks later, a tenant moved in, and I never heard a complaint.

I will share a warning about the ozone machine: make sure you do your research on possible health risks associated with its use.

Vinegar and baking soda mixed in a spray bottle – Vinegar is an amazing stain remover, good for blood, urine, etc. and baking soda is a fantastic odor remover. When they're mixed together, they make a perfect combo of odor remover and stain remover.

Hydrogen peroxide and baking soda – This is great for removing urine smells (hopefully from pets, but not limited). Hydrogen Peroxide is great for breaking down the crystals of urine; baking soda is great for the removal of odor.

Citrus – Enzyme Cleaner – This sounds very scientific, but it's a really simple home remedy that works well. All you need to do is put water, orange peel scraps, and brown sugar in a bottle. Shake it up, release the cap, retighten, and leave for a few months. Then your enzyme cleaner/odor remover will be ready to use.

Citrus Peels – Citrus peels make a great deodorizer. They work best in more localized spaces like closets. You just need to place the peels in the affected area for a few days.

Baking Soda – Baking soda is an amazing odor remover. You can buy it in boxes. If you have a fridge that smells, open a box and place it in the fridge or freezer. This is something you should definitely do if the unit is empty and has no power. You can also place open boxes in other smelly rooms, or sprinkle it on a smelly carpet. Baking soda will absorb the smell.

Vinegar – Vinegar to cleaners is like duct tape to tape. It can be used for cleaning and deodorizing just about anything.

Bleach – Bleach can have its own strong odor, so be careful when using pure bleach. It's an amazing cleaner and deodorizer. It works exceptionally well in bathrooms not only for the sink, tub, and toilet but also for getting mold and mildew off shower curtains, tiles, and grout. You can mix it with water and put it in a spray bottle to control the use a bit better. You also need to keep it away from colored fabrics, carpets, and clothing. It can leave white spots. It also has a tendency to absorb into your skin, so make sure to wear gloves. Don't use bleach with ammonia, hydrogen peroxide, or several other household cleaners, especially if they contain ammonia or peroxide. The reason is that you will create a poisonous gas called chloramine. This gas can cause some or all of the following: Chest pain, watery eyes, shortness of breath, and the possibility of more serious illness. As long as you use bleach properly, it will leave a nice clean smell instead of a foul odor.

Ammonia – You can use ammonia to remove paint smells from rooms. Although, in the rental business, sometimes, the smell of fresh paint can be a selling feature of a unit. But if a tenant complains or it's too strong, place a bowl of ammonia in the affected room. Ammonia can also be used to remove smells related to mold and mildew. It's important to keep ammonia away from bleach or cleaners containing bleach. It's equivalent to using bleach and can be very effective; just never use them together.

Onion slices – onions can be great to absorb bacteria and odors. They can work well if you have a room with a strong paint smell. All you need to do is cut an onion in half and place it in the room with the odor.

If you cut the onion up into small pieces, it can be more effective; however, the room may smell of onions.

Dryer sheets (most common type is Bounce) – they can be used to absorb foul odors in rooms. They're great for smoke. Perfect to place in closets, bathrooms, and let them do the work.

Charcoal – You can buy charcoal, where you buy fish aquarium supplies. Aquariums use charcoal filters. Charcoal can be a cheap nontoxic odor remover.

Air Sponge – there's a product you can buy called an air sponge. What it does is absorb odors into a gel-type substance. They come ready to use. Just remove the cover and place in the room.

Clearing Slow and Clogged Drains

When you have tenants, you cannot control what might end up in your drains. There are several drains in every rental unit, toilet, sinks, tubs, and shower drains. Even if you have a great plumber on speed dial, it's important for every landlord/property manager to have an understanding of how to unclog a drain.

When you have new tenants you need to educate them on what should never go in a drain and how to use a plunger. Some items to tell them to never put in a drain or toilet are as follows: Baby wipes, bacon fat, cooking grease, oil, and petroleum based products, drano or other acid-based clog removers, utensils, paper towels, feminine hygiene products, thick toilet paper, or anything that will not dissolve or break down quickly.

Garbage disposal – if the unit has a garbage disposal, let your tenants know not to put utensils, dishcloths, rice, pasta, celery, asparagus, or broken glass or china in the garbage disposal.

Don't assume something is common sense.

The following is the minimum you need to know about drains:

Drano – or acid-based drain cleaner – I have to admit I'm guilty of using Drano before to get a drain flowing again. It can be effective in the short term. I don't recommend that you use it. Chemical drain cleaners are full of acid. The acid breaks down the blockage and the drain then flows free again. The problem is that the acid can also harm the pipes. The acid can also eat human skin. It can be a hazard if it's put into a drain, doesn't work, and you call a plumber or another person to help. That plumber or person may use a plunger or remove the cap on a sink P-trap to get rid of the clog. They might be unaware of the acid drain cleaner. It could splash on their skin and cause a permanent scar, or make holes in clothing. My advice would be to avoid chemical drain clog removers.

P-Trap If you look under a sink you will see a curved pipe, at the base of the curve there will be a removable cap. If you have a clogged sink, you can remove the cap over a bucket and, often, you will have a bunch of debris fall out. I have had small toys, hair, jewelry, dishcloths, utensils, and, of course, food come out. After it's clear, you can just screw the cap back on and the drain should flow.

Plunger – In all your units, a good investment is a plunger for every toilet. It doesn't cost much and can save you some service calls. A plunger can also work in a sink and tub as well as toilets. You should know how to use a plunger and educate your tenants on how to use one.

Snake / Roto-rooter – A snake is basically a metal cable with a handle on it. They come in various lengths and thicknesses, some attach to the end of drills, and most plumbers have bigger and longer ones that mount on a spool (like a garden hose). The plumber's version will usually operate by electricity. The commercial versions will have different attachments to cut through different clogs. You can buy the smaller ones in the plumbing section of most hardware or department store. The small ones can be good for smaller clogs that aren't too far from your access point. You may need a commercial version if the clog is out to the middle of the front lawn. Also, if the clog is a tree root, you'll need a heavy-duty Roto-rooter. To access a commercial version, you will need to hire a plumber who has one, or rent one.

Grow Ops

A grow op is where someone rents a house or apartment for the purpose of growing marijuana. That might not sound like a big deal; however, it's very destructive to buildings. Some grow ops cause less damage than others. It can completely destroy a house, and, depending on your insurance policy, you may not be covered for all the damage. If you live in a city or area where it's common, make sure you have a grow op discussion with your insurance broker.

When marijuana is grown, the plants need to be kept moist and warm. Most of the damage is caused by moisture that leads to mold and mildew that soaks into the walls. So, a lot of times, if there was a grow op in the unit, the drywall may need to be replaced. The problem with grow ops is the growers will keep the plants moist and warm, and the weed-smelling moisture gets absorbed by drywall. A grow op can be a major problem for landlords and property managers.

Another common problem is the criminals will alter the plumbing and electrical systems to fabricate make-shift sprinklers to keep the plants watered.

The good news is that power companies will investigate homes with extremely high spikes in power consumption. It can take a lot of electricity to run the lights to keep the plants warm. The challenge with this is that some criminals have figured out how to tap directly into a power pole or neighboring homes.

You might not be able to screen your way out of a grow op situation. The criminals will either pose as fine respectable people, or hire other people to meet with you to rent the place. That's why you need to do your best screening. Many landlords get burned by being fooled by a well-dressed couple who show up in a decent car, and have all the right answers. You need to do a proper background check on everyone. You need to take a copy of ID when you're signing a lease. I will agree that if they're pros, they might get through your screening process, but here's a reality check to all the small, independent landlords.

They're looking for you. They look for houses where the owner needs to leave town, but either doesn't want to sell their home or cannot. These people often are too cheap to hire a professional property manager, so they meet with a respectable-looking couple who pay on time, and they leave town. Since no one is checking on the house and the rent is always paid, these make perfect houses for grow ops. They load the house with plants, and modify whatever way necessary to help the plants grow.

The unsuspecting landlord will usually only find out when it's too late. The criminals grow the plants, harvest the crop. At that point they will either start growing a new crop or move onto to a new house. All of a sudden, the rent doesn't show up. The landlord either checks on the property or has someone else check on it, and they find the damage. If you're going to rent your house and leave town, even if you chose not to hire a property manager, it's important that you have someone you trust check on the property. You need someone to drive by and do a visual. Does it looked lived in? Are there ever any cars in the driveway? Are they the same cars? Are the curtains always closed? Is the lawn mowed? Then, at the very least, even if everything looks fine, you need to have someone enter the house. You will have to give the tenant proper notice. If you provide notice and gain access only to find your suspicions are correct, you should immediately contact the police.

I interviewed a real estate investor who is also a plumber. He got a great deal on a former grow op property. It was the straw that broke the camel's back for a lady who owned a property for many years. What happened was the landlady allowed a tenant to sublet an attic apartment in a house for the summer while the tenant was away. It was to another student, and this landlady let her guard down and allowed the sublet to take place without doing much screening. The sublet started a grow op in the attic. This particular criminal did damage to the electrical and plumbing and caused a mold problem. This particular landlady didn't want to spend any more money on the house or deal with the stress of being a landlady, so she sold the house to my investor friend. He ended up getting a great deal, since he was able to do most of the repairs himself.

The bottom line is that you need to be aware that it could happen to one of your rentals. It's important to screen and keep a close watch on your investment properties.

Renovations on the Cheap

When you're renovating properties and getting them ready for tenants, sometimes, speed and cost are big factors. I want to share some cheap fixes that work great if you need to get a unit ready for a tenant. Some of these fixes are not super long term, but will work in the short term. I'm sure there are many more, but these are the ones we use on a regular basis.

Kitchen:

Kitchen in a box. This is a great way to remodel a kitchen on a budget. These have become really popular over the past five years. Basically, you measure the wall space in your kitchen. Then go to a local hardware store. Ask for premade cabinets. You can buy them white, stained, or unfinished. They come in various sizes, for top and bottom. You measure what you need, and have them cut you a countertop. Then take them to your unit, and, in one day, you can have a new kitchen.

Kitchen reface – we have a guy who will replace all the cupboard doors, and the fronts of the drawers. This is a great way to give a kitchen a brand new look at a fraction of the cost of replacing it. They make use of the existing boxes.

139

Cupboard hardware and paint – sometimes all it takes is a fresh coat of paint and some new door and drawer handles to make kitchen cupboards look new. You can use melamine paint, or chalk paint, then dress it up with some new handles and knobs.

Wrong ordered cabinets – If you go to a kitchen cabinet store or the kitchen section of a building supply store, you can often find cabinets that were made to the wrong specs or a certain project. They will sell these for a significantly discounted price.

Bathroom:

Vanity in a box – you can dress up a bathroom by buying a new sink and vanity. You may even be able to use the old taps. These ready-to-use sinks and vanities or pedestal sinks can be found for a low price (often on sale) at most hardware and building supply stores.

Bathtub reglazing – There are several companies around that will do bathtub re-glazing. Basically, what they do is repaint the tub. It can make a tired old tub look new for a fraction of the cost of replacement, plus the process can be completed in one day. In our experience, the glazing will start to peel, but not for two to three years.

Bathtub and surround covers – there are companies that will install a new tub and tub surround over the existing one all in one day. They will also install new taps. This process is not cheap, but the time it saves by not having to do a demolition, is well worth it.

Mirror – If you want to modernize your bathroom, it can be a good idea to remove the old medicine cabinet and install a large wall-mounted mirror in its place.

Flooring:

Peel and stick – peel and stick products have greatly improved over the past few years. We have used peel and stick laminate wood-looking flooring in many rooms. We have also used some peel and stick tiles that you would swear were ceramic. The great thing is that peel and stick doesn't take much talent or special skill to install. It's also quick and ready to use, so it can be a great way to make a unit look fresh and new in a short time.

Dap or white silicone – This is a painter's and renovator's best friend. If you have baseboards that have gaps in the corners or against the wall, you can fill it with dap and paint over it. You can also use it to fill nail and screw holes in walls, and cracks in walls. Dap or white silicone can cover up many imperfections and make a place look great.

Window Coverings:

Inexpensive blinds – When we renovate a place, we'll buy cheap blinds for the windows at the front of the property. It's a great value add for your tenants, and doesn't cost very much money.

Curtains – Curtains and curtain rods can be purchased for a low price, we install them in the living room windows of our properties. It's a low-priced value add, and will avoid the risk of your new tenants using a bed sheet for privacy.

Landscaping:

Bark mulch – this is a landlord's best friend. You can add significant curb appeal to a property by cleaning out weeds in planters and replacing them with bark mulch. It's relatively inexpensive and will look great.

Good grass seed – This may seem counterintuitive to do when you're saving money, but buy good grass seed. The more expensive grass seed will grow well, even if the soil beneath it isn't that great. You can make a crappy old lawn look lush and green in a matter of weeks.

The Real Deal on Hiring Contractors

We've been renovating properties for close to 15 years. We've used the same contractors for several projects, we've had to let some go, and some moved away. Some did crappy work, so we didn't rehire.

We have hired people for small, medium, and large jobs. I want to write about hiring contractors with a bit of a twist. The theory

I've read about hiring contractors doesn't line up with the reality. Most of the articles I've read also don't explain the size of the contract. I've also noticed most articles don't talk about timeline or availability of contractors willing and able to do the job.

I want to let all the property managers, builders, landlords, developers, investors, and flippers know that if you can't seem to get the theory you've read to match up to your reality, you're not alone.

Here's the advice that's usually written (or some version similar to the following):

Part 1 – Always make sure to hire a contractor with reliable references. Confirm that it was done well, on time, and on budget.

Part 2 – Get three detailed quotes. Compare based on time, materials, and price.

Part 3 – Make sure you get a performance guarantee in writing. Make sure the contractor has proper insurance and pays into workers compensation.

Part 4 – Don't pay for work in advance, unless it's a large project. Even on a large project, don't pay more than one third of the project in advance.

Part 5 – Make sure to have a penalty discount in place for delays or incomplete work.

I know many of you are likely thinking, *that all sounds reasonable.* You may have even read similar advice. I would have to agree that it's great advice, but it lacks context. In the property management, flipping, land lording, and development business, projects come in all shapes, sizes, and costs. You may have a contractor involved in something from as small as replacing a light fixture to something as big as constructing an apartment building. The budget for a renovation could range from under one hundred dollars to hundreds of thousands of dollars.

Well, here it is: the real deal:

Part 1: References – yes, word of mouth is usually the best way. I agree that you absolutely should use someone who comes recommended by someone who has used them. One of the best sources is a local real estate group. I've met some fantastic contractors in the local real estate group I attend. Talk to people who have used them. However, here's the deal. Make sure they do the type of work you're looking to get done. If they specialize and exclusively build million dollar homes, you would likely not hire them to renovate a kitchen or basic bungalow. I would be reluctant to hire a contractor without a recommendation from someone you know. If you're new to an area and are dealing with a realtor, home inspector, etc., they should have the name of at least one good contractor. It's also a good idea to google the contractor's name and check the better business bureau. The other thing to remember is that good contractors are usually busy, so the more notice you can give them of your upcoming project, the better. When you're talking to references, keep an open mind around questions related to budget. A lot of times, it's the client who adds to the project's budget and timeline.

Part 2: Get three detailed quotes – This might be a challenge. There are a few variables involved in this process. If you expect to google three local contractors, call them up, and they're going to run over and do a detailed quote, I think you'll be disappointed. That's why Part 1 is so important. If you're a real estate investor, you need to use some estimating tricks to have an idea about how much renovations cost. For example, you can estimate labor based on the cost of an item. For example, a bathtub may cost $300 and rule-of-thumb labor estimate would be $300, so the project would cost approximately $600. The other factor will be the size of the project. If you're trying to get one door, a kitchen countertop, and a few other minor repairs done, I wouldn't beat yourself up if you cannot find three contractors to come give you an estimate. If you're planning a major renovation, you may need some time and patience to find three contractors to give you proper estimates. It sounds like it would be easy to do, but it's a major challenge for most of the people I work with. What I would recommend is forming a relationship with a great general contractor. That way, you'll have someone willing to work with you on small and large projects. I would also form a separate relationship with a painter, electrician, plumber, and handyman, so that you'll have a person on your team to handle any size project or maintenance issue. The bottom line is that if you're finding it hard or impossible to get three written quotes from contractors, that's more the norm.

The part about materials is going to be up to you. If you want to invest in real estate, you need to educate yourself on what materials cost. All materials can vary in cost. An obvious one would be a granite countertop compared to laminate; however, in some cases, some cheaper materials can take just as much or more labor to install. An example might be ceramic tile versus a laminate floor that may take just as much time for an experienced tile installer. You don't have to know the exact cost to do projects; however, as an expert, you will be required to do some research and learn from experience. That way, if a contractor quotes you $2,000 to install a basic steel door, you will know that either some major work needs to be done around the doorframe, or you're being overcharged. The same can be said if someone quotes you $200 to install a steel door, you know that either they're dealing with stolen building supplies, or they're going to ask for the money up front, and you'll never see them again.

Part 3: Make sure you get a performance guarantee in writing; make sure the contractor has proper insurance and pays into workers' compensation – Workers' compensation and liability insurance are important for your contractors to have. It's a good idea to make sure they have proper insurance, including errors and omissions, general liability, and workers' compensation, especially if they're hiring subcontractors to help. A performance guarantee would usually only apply if the project were large (maybe $100K plus). In most cases, projects of any size will come with a written estimate and a discussed timeline. I find that sometimes, contracts get delayed for various reasons. It could be a material delay, a subcontractor, a major surprise, which often happen when you're working on old buildings. It's important to realize that if you're going to be in the real estate investment business, surprizes happen. The best contractor in the world cannot predict surprises, such as asbestos or knob and tube electrical hidden in the walls. In one project we were doing, our electrician discovered zero insulation in a couple of walls. When we bought the house, we did a few test holes and found insulation, so we were surprised. You could also get a permit delay from the city. It's important to be reasonable with the contractor you hire. If you blame them and refuse to pay any extra for a surprise problem, you'll likely start a dispute, which will cost you time and money. I will also admit that we've hired the odd contractor to do a small project like one door or some miscellaneous repairs and didn't check for insurance. We just paid cash. I don't recommend this, especially for jobs over $2500, but it's pretty common in our business.

Part 4: Don't pay for work in advance, unless it's a large project – The subject of payment needs context. If you're hiring a handyman or small contractor to do a small job like replace one door or lay down a couple floors, they may want you to pay for the supplies up front. That can be okay. I would be reluctant to pay for any of the labor up front, but be prepared to pay immediately when the job is done, especially if you're going to hire them again. If you're doing a larger project with a larger company, they will likely not ask you for much money up front. I even had one contractor tell me to make sure I never hire a flat broke contractor. A larger company will usually ask for installments, especially if they're providing subcontractor labor and materials. I would never pay in full until the contract was complete. You need to have some leverage. If you're dealing with a reputable contractor, they will not ask for a final payment until the job is done and you're happy.

Part 5: Make sure to have a penalty discount in place for delays or incomplete work – This is advice that I often hear, but I'm not sure who follows it. The most predictable thing about construction and renovations is that it's unpredictable. We have renovated several old buildings over the years and performed lots of various maintenance projects on old buildings. Surprises happen. If you're doing a new build of an apartment building, and the project is several hundred thousand or millions of dollars, then I would put some rewards or penalties in place. The final payment will not be required until the job is done, so that should be incentive to have the job completed. I think for the average project, if you started talking about a penalty based on performance, you may scare several contractors away.

In summary, in my opinion, it's important to build a relationship with a contractor who will treat you well, charge you a fair price, and be there for you when you need them. They also should have an understanding of what your project goal is. You need a contractor who understands that time is money. They need to understand the importance of timelines and the kind of work you expect.

As the client, you need to realize that all clients are different; your standards may be different from every other client they worked with. In my opinion, many disputes could be avoided or resolved with better communication between the client and contractor. I hope I've been able to add some perspective to common contractor hiring advice.

Should You Allow Your Tenants to Paint?

This is a subject we get asked about a lot. We often get asked by new tenants if they can paint; we also have landlords and property managers asking what we do. This topic has to be addressed every time we have a tenant turnover.

I'm going to share with you four stories, then I'll tell you our current position. The stories will show you how we arrived at our current position, and you can take it from there.

Story 1: Adding color to a multi-family – Several years ago, we purchased an apartment building. There were a few vacant units when we closed on the property. We had also just completed a renovation on a personal property. This meant we had various colors of paint. In our personal house, we don't like to have just one color. This gave me an idea. I felt that the units in this building were in good condition; however, they seemed boring. They were off-white. Not quite white and not quite beige. I decided I would paint the apartments I was redoing with our leftover paint. I thought I was taking a stand against boring apartments. I figured I would be making a difference in people's lives.

Here's how it actually turned out. Everyone I showed the apartments to complained about the colors. I didn't have one person say, "Wow, awesome paint," or "Great job." Even my superintendent questioned my judgement.

I did manage to get tenants for the apartments, but I had to paint them a new color. I bought a five-gallon bucket of high quality, one coat paint. I named my new color *renters' beige*. It's actually a really nice non-offensive color that most people seem to like.

I talked to other landlords about painting apartments and if we should allow our tenants to paint. I have to agree, that if you're dealing with apartments in regular buildings, you should include painting in your "make ready" process.

The time spent may depend on how fast you need to turn over the unit, and what the history of the tenure of the tenants is in the building.

There are three ways to paint an apartment:

- **Deluxe** – a deluxe paint job is where the baseboards, trim, and ceiling are all painted white, and the walls are a different color.

- **Basic Paint job** – a basic paint job is where the ceiling is white and the trim and baseboards are the same color as the walls.

- **Quick and dirty** – a quick and dirty paint job is where the ceiling, walls, trim, and baseboards are all one color.

I would suggest using a light beige; however, I did see a recent headline on an article and it read something like this: **Notice to landlords from your tenants, put down the beige paint and back away slowly**. That may be an indication that beige is being played out.

Story 2: The sports fan – I got this story from a landlord in a meetup group I belong to. The landlord didn't know about it until the tenant moved out (they did a midnight move). When this landlord went to inspect the apartment, it had one wall in the master bedroom dedicated to the Toronto Maple Leafs. The whole wall was a logo. I'm sure you can see some obvious problems with this. The background to the logo is dark blue. It took a lot of paint to cover up this logo. This situation may have been unavoidable, however. My landlord friend had to admit he didn't discuss paint when the tenant moved in. This particular tenant

ended up skipping out on rent, so it wasn't something he could deduct from the damage deposit. If you run into this type of situation, it's important to tell the tenant before the final inspection how much will be deducted from the damage deposit. Providing a specific amount may encourage the tenant to do the painting themselves, or they may decide to leave it. Either way, it will prevent any surprises.

Story 3: My tenants only thought they knew how to paint – We rented a house to a family a few years back. I will say they were great tenants other than this one thing. When they moved in, it was a situation where the other tenants were moving out at the same time they were coming in. We didn't have time to paint. Now, the place didn't look too bad, but the tenant moving out had been there for a couple of years, so a couple of rooms could have used a refresh. The new tenants didn't mind, but they asked if they were allowed to paint. We said, "Yes, you do the work, and we'll pay for the paint." I sometimes forget and I don't want to brag, but Shelly and I are really good at cutting in. We don't use tape and our paint jobs always look great. We just assumed that everyone else would be as good or use tape until they get the experience required to do a great job. In the case of this house, when I was doing the move out preinspection, I realized that my tenants didn't know how to paint. They only painted a few rooms, but the cutting in job where the walls met the ceiling was terrible. It may have been one of the worst cut in jobs, I've ever seen. The lesson learned from this story is that if a tenant asks if they can paint, it is important to ask about their painting experience and what colors they're going to use.

Story 4: The double paint job – We aim to give every apartment a fresh coat of paint before a new tenant moves in. We hire a painter to do the work. In our area, you can get a two-bedroom apartment painted for $400 to $500 or more if all the trim and baseboards need to be done. We provide the paint. Most professional painters usually bring their own brush. This is a story of a bit of miscommunication. The tenants viewed the apartment before they moved in and asked about the painting policy. Shelly explained it to them, and asked if they were interested in painting the apartment themselves. The current tenant had moved out early, so we had agreed to give them the place early for them to paint. They filled out an application and accepted the apartment. They decided they would rather have us paint the apartment before they moved in, so we did. They lived in the apartment for about three months, then they called Shelly and asked if she would still honor the deal where we pay for the paint and they do the work. Shelly and I had to weigh the pros and cons. The upside is that these tenants were happy, did a great job painting, and stayed another couple of years.

Where we stand today: I can sum it up in three sections – Timing, expectations, and budget.

Timing: this is always a challenge in our business. We want to turn apartments over quickly so we don't lose revenue. We also like to have a fresh coat of paint on the walls before we do the move-in inspection. That's the theory; however, we all know that theory and reality are often two different things. I find that even if you have to do some painting after a tenant moves in, they're generally understanding. If the unit you're renting is a house/apartment, you may want to talk to your tenants about the painting. We notice on apartments and houses, the people looking for this type of accommodation are a bit fussier about paint color. I will have to leave it on this thought. Shoot for the ideal, but be willing to negotiate timing of paint with your tenant.

Expectations: One of the main reasons we like to have an apartment fully painted before a tenant moves in, is that it demonstrates how we would like the apartment to look at all times. If you don't do the painting, it makes your move-in inspection more difficult, and could set the expectation that paint and cleanliness is not a big deal. The other side also is that the tenant may think you're lazy and don't care. That could be a red flag for your potential tenants. The bottom line is that whatever you decide, it's important that you and your tenant understand the expectations of each other in regards to the painting.

Budget: there are two parts to this. One is your apartment turnover side. The stage is set in our area for how much a painter can charge to paint an apartment. Unless they're doing something special, the market price exists. We always buy 5-gallon buckets of the same color paint, so we have some available at all times. The other part is that if you allow your tenants to paint and agree to pay for supplies, explain what that means. Get a quote in advance. We've been caught off guard with receipts sent to us for expensive paint brushes and high-end paint. You can also set a maximum limit, and tell them you will pay up to that amount. Then, if they want to use expensive paint, they still can.

The apartment rental business is competitive, so we feel it's important to be flexible. The key is in communication. Make sure you and your tenant are on the same page.

How to Avoid the $10-Per-Hour Property Management Jobs

Guilty as charged. Shelly and I are sometimes guilty of doing the $10-per-hour property management jobs. What I mean by the $10-per-hour jobs are all the jobs that you know you should hire people to do, but you find yourself attracted to in the name of saving cash, improving cash flow, etc.

Here's the story that has lead us to significantly minimize the amount of them we do.

When we first started investing in real estate, we were into buying older properties, living in and renovating them, and then selling for a profit. It was rewarding, stressful, and tiring. We would work our day jobs all day, then go home at night and work on our house. We went through several years of living in renovation projects. We did everything we could to avoid paying someone else to work for us. We would sacrifice our own mental well-being to save a dollar.

This included painting, plumbing, flooring, junk removal, landscaping, etc. I can remember spending every moment we had off work, working on one of our projects. We learned a lot but, basically, had no life, except between projects.

We eventually changed our investment strategy to a buy and hold formula. We tried to do the work ourselves, but, by this time, we had a child plus demanding jobs. I will admit that I find something therapeutic about doing manual labor, but we have minimized the small jobs we do.

A conversation I had with an experienced investor one day changed my outlook for good. He basically said, focus on what you're good at, and let the professionals do what they're good at. He said if I wanted any kind of peace of mind in this business, I would have to stop doing the $10-per-hour jobs.

You see, at that point, I realized I was better off focusing on my day job, and finding and funding projects, rather than trying to fit working on the project into my already jammed schedule. He said my focus shouldn't be on just adding to my portfolio with buildings, but adding systems to handle the extra buildings without increasing my workload.

I found that changing my mindset saved time and allowed me to think more clearly, which has led to more money and peace of mind.

Here's my advice:

When you're building a real estate portfolio, make sure you're building systems at the same time.

Make sure to always have a professional handyman who can handle small jobs on speed dial. This is one of the most valuable members of your team. You may think you're saving money by driving out to a property on a weekend or after work, but believe me, your time is better spent planning your next project, spending time with family, or whatever you do to relax.

If you want to make your life even easier, hire a professional property manager.

Plan your projects right to the smallest detail. If you don't delegate tasks like cleaning a job site, hanging blinds, or placing and hooking up appliances, then you'll likely find yourself doing those $10 dollar-per-hour jobs yourself. Even if you have to pay $20 or $30 per hour, you'll still be further ahead hiring someone to do them.

With the systems we have in place, we don't do too many $10 dollar-per-hour jobs. I just want to make sure you don't beat yourself up by occasionally doing a small job or taking care of a small tenant issue.

Keep a Close Watch on Utility Bills

When I got into multifamily investing, I learned very quickly that the old saying "a penny saved is a penny earned" applies to property management. One of the most important reasons to have your property professionally managed is to watch the expenses.

Some of the basics are doing routine inspections every six months or, at the very least, once per year. It's important to focus on preventative maintenance. It's better to have a proactive mindset, rather than a reactive mindset.

Another area you can save money is to watch for inconsistencies in any of the utility bills you pay. It's common in our area to pay the water bill for your properties. In the Halifax area, even if you transfer the water bill into your tenant's name, if they don't pay, the landlord will be required to pick up the bill. That's why most landlords include it in the rent, at no extra cost.

Yesterday, we noticed a problem with a water bill at one of our properties. The usage was double the previous month. That indicated a problem. Either the tenant was suddenly using much more water, or there was a leak.

We immediately sent our handyman to investigate. He discovered that the bathtub tap was leaking. He replaced the cartridge, and the problem was solved. This simple fix will save us a lot of money over time.

We had a power bill problem a few years ago that we were able to fix. We had made a deal with a tenant to have power included in the rent. It was okay at first, but when it got cold, the power bill went sky high. We had our property manager talk to the tenant. When he arrived, the thermostats were on 25 degrees Celsius (77 degree Fahrenheit), and I mean all of them. Every room. What we decided to do was set up programmable thermostats. We didn't just install them and leave; we had our electrician set them all up based around the tenant's work schedule. This proved to be an easy fix that saved us hundreds of dollars.

If you're paying any of the utilities at your properties, make sure to check for inconsistencies.

These are just a couple of examples where you can save/earn more money. Make sure to check all your bills related to each property to maximize your cash flow.

Flags in the Window

Have you ever driven by a house or apartment building and seen a flag or a sheet used as a curtain. I'm sure most of you will agree that it takes away from the curb appeal.

I might be half or fully crazy, but it's definitely a pet peeve of mine. I know most people will make it a building rule to not allow flags or sheets as curtains, but let's face it; it could be a low priority on a tenant's list. They may move in and have a new job, school registration, general unpacking, etc. to do. The purchase of curtains and blinds may be something they plan to do in the next week. Then we can all relate to how a week can turn into a month, etc.

We've come up with an easy, inexpensive solution to this problem, which you may want to adopt. In the past few years, the price of blinds has come down significantly, plus there are a few extra inexpensive options on the market. What we do is install blinds in the street-facing windows of our apartments.

You can get a decent blind that looks great for $8 to $10. Here are some of the benefits of this small investment:

1. No more driving by and seeing sheets, flags, towels, etc. used as curtains.
2. Better curb appeal – your rental property will look better.
3. Security – gives the appearance that the unit is occupied.
4. If you're showing a vacant unit, the blinds make the apartment look cleaner.
5. Value added service for your tenants. All of our tenants really appreciate having blinds on the street-facing windows in place when they move in.

I hope you'll help us end the unsightly practice of using sheets, towels, flags, etc. for curtains.

Cold-Weather Lock and Door Maintenance

Winter in Nova Scotia gets cold, really cold, and snowy. That can cause a problem for both tenants and owners. We get at least one call every year about a door that won't close.

I've seen some cases where, the smallest piece of ice will cause a door not to close. I've gained experience over the years, so I now know what to look for if I get a call about a door not closing in the winter.

In one case, there were a couple of issues and Shelly and I had to bring a hair dryer, a knife, and a towel (the towel was used to clean up when we were done).

Here's what happened. We had a lot of snow and cold (-10 degree C) weather. The snow and ice built up around the edge, and under the door. Also, the weather seal around the door had ice buildup.

We used a knife to scrape away the larger chunks of ice, then we used a hair dryer to melt the rest of the ice around the door. When we were finished, the door closed perfectly.

This particular case was easy to solve. But not all frozen door problems can be solved like this.

Here are some examples of other problems and possible solutions:

Key will not go into lock – Sometimes, moisture will get inside the door lock and not only prevent the door from opening properly, but causing the door to not open at all. You can usually get into the lock quickly with either lock de-icer or pour a hot cup of water over the lock (warning the water will freeze again, this is a quick temporary solution) This will get you in, but won't solve the problem. What you want to look for is a way that the water got in. Now, it could be just a one-time deal, or water could be getting in behind the lock. You can use silicone around the edge of the lock to prevent water from getting in again. You can also use a silicone lubricant or similar product and spray it into the lock to prevent a future problem.

Door will not close, but no ice around the door – This problem can be a bit tougher to solve when it's very cold out. We've seen doors expand, preventing the door from opening or closing. We've seen this with older doors that have metal on the outside and wood on the inside and around the edges. When you run into this problem, you will need to make a judgement call. The door could be old and starting to fall apart (leaving gaps for water to enter). If this is the case, you can start with your heat gun (or dryer) and try to thaw the door. You can also use a bit of force with a hammer (only if the door is close to the end of its usable life). Shelly and I had a door in the back of a house once that we had to leave closed for the winter. It became extremely hard to open and close as soon as it got cold. If the door is the main or only entrance to an apartment, then replacing the door and frame may be necessary.

The reality is that in colder climates, you may not be able to avoid a frozen door complaint. It's also important to realize a tiny piece of ice in the wrong place can cause a door not to close. Try to educate the users of the door about clearing all snow away from it.

Another solution to a problem door is to shave a bit off the bottom of the door or doorframe. Then add some flexible weather stripping to fill in any gaps.

I hope this section provide you with some guidance on what to do when a door will not open or close.

Who Should Mow the Lawn or Shovel Snow?

This question can be answered a few different ways. I'll tell you what we do, and you can decide what works best for you.

The short answer is: it depends.

If the property has five or more units, I would suggest you hire someone to do it.

If the property is a single-family house, I would suggest you have the tenant do it.

There are a couple of exceptions. If you have a building with 5 or more units, you might have an eager tenant or superintendent who is willing to do the lawn care and snow removal, or one or the other.

If you're renting a high-end single-family home, you may include snow removal and lawn care in the rent. That will be a personal decision.

The grey area is about the buildings with between 2 and 5 units. This is where there are several answers. I solve this problem on a case-by-case basis.

I will share some examples:

We have a four-unit property with a large yard. I hire someone to do the lawn and snow removal at this property.

We have a triplex where one of the tenants does the mowing with a mower we've provided and we hire someone to plow the driveway.

We have an over/under set of apartments, where the person in the upper unit mows with their own mower and the tenants individually do their own snow removal.

I have another over/under set of apartments where one of the previous tenants used to mow the lawn for a rent reduction. I provided the mower. When they moved out, they asked if they could come back and do it. They've been moving the lawn there ever since. I pay them to do it. We just worked out a deal. They really enjoy mowing and making a bit of cash, so it is a win-win. At this particular building, the tenants take care of the snow removal.

I have a single-family house where the tenant was responsible for the lawn care but never mowed the lawn. I never received any complaints from by-law enforcement (they will contact you as the owner), so I never said anything for a while. Then they moved out, and I had to hire a company to cut the grass before I could show it to potential tenants. This has been a challenge that I've come across a few times. You need to be aware if you leave snow and lawn care up to the tenant, they may not do it to your standard.

That may or may not become an issue, depending on the neighborhood. In my experience, all the tenants who agree to handle the lawn care seem to take pride in doing it. This is, of course, with some exceptions like the story I just shared.

Many investors suggest hiring pros so that your place will always look great. In my opinion, it's often hard to find reliable snow removal and lawn mowing companies. I have tried several, and have fired companies over the years for not showing up. If you have a large budget, some of the big companies with lots of staff can be a lot more reliable, but they come with a big price tag.

We do it on a building-by-building basis and formulate a plan that works for the particular property. When I first started out in the landlord business, I used to do a few myself. I found it too time consuming, so I stopped doing that after a couple of years.

Shelly painting

CHAPTER 10 - BUGS AND RODENTS

"We are what we repeatedly do. Excellence,
then, is not an act, but a habit" —Aristotle

If you own or manage properties, you'll end up dealing with bugs and rodents. There are different types of rodents and insects depending on where you live. Some areas are better or worse, some pests are poisonous or just annoying.

Some examples of insects are ants, cockroaches, earwigs, termites, sow bugs, scorpions, fleas, spiders, crickets, beetles, June bugs, bed bugs,silver fish, bees, hornets and wasps..

Some examples of pesky animals are as follows: raccoons, skunks, porcupines, mice, rats, squirrels, armadillos, ground hogs, garden snakes, rattlesnakes, alligators, and crocodiles.

It's a good idea to hire a professional to get rid of pest problems in your properties. Many companies will offer one-time solutions, but most will offer you a contract, where for a monthly fee, they make sure you don't have any pest problems on or in your property. If you have a property greater than 6 units or in an area prone to the above list of potential problems, you will more than likely need a monthly maintenance plan. A common rate for a one-time deal is about $200. That's also around what a monthly contract will cost, but it will depend on the area.

Bugs and rodents can bring down the value of your property and cause good tenants to leave. It's important to take complaints from tenants seriously. I've solved pest problems on my own and also by hiring professionals.

I cannot speak on how to eradicate all the above issues; however, I think I can provide value with some stories.

Attack of the Fleas

"Oh no, we have a major flea problem." That's what I said a few years back when I started a renovation project on a recently purchased two-unit property. I've seen fleas before and have had to deal with them on my cats over the years.

I've never really considered them a major problem until my electricians walked off the job. They said they wouldn't come back until I dealt with the problem. I just figured they were exaggerating and blowing the situation out of proportion. Maybe they had blood that attracted fleas.

Well, I have to admit, I had to eat crow. My handyman/painter met me at the property to investigate. We put on white painter coveralls and entered the property.

The property was completely vacant, no furniture, carpets, or curtains. We were only in the house for a few minutes when fleas started appearing all over our white coveralls. It was as if we were being attacked. I quickly realized our electricians weren't exaggerating about the flea situation.

At that point, our handyman/painter said, "You're on your own." He didn't want to bring fleas home. I was left alone to figure out a solution. I made a few calls to some experienced friends and found out the best way to deal with the situation was with flea bombs.

A flea bomb is a can that you set in the middle of the room, press a button, and run. It fills the room and kills the fleas. The problem is, since there were likely unhatched eggs, I had to come back a couple of days later and do it again.

I was also fortunate, because our partner Mike Thibeau had just flown into town, so I was able to enlist his help with the flea bombs. We had to do it to the upper and lower units.

This method of extermination worked very well; we completed the process twice to make sure we got them all. It took about four days, but we seemed to eliminate all the fleas.

We managed to get our electricians and handyman/painter back on site, and finished the project.

Bees / Hornets and Wasps

Bees can be a problem for both noise and the fact that they can sting, so they terrify many people.

If bees are on the outside, you can get a beekeeper to remove them and some will do it for free. If their on the inside, that's not possible. Also, the sooner you call the exterminator the better. If they have time to start a honeycomb, the honey will attract another bee colony and you may have to cut the wall to remove the comb. Also, when you caulk the hole, make sure the caulk doesn't shrink leaving a gap that bees can get through. That happened to a friend of mine, so he sprayed and recaulked, but the bees survived and found their way into the house. He had to set off foggers and spend the night in a hotel.

You can get rid of hornets and wasps in a similar way, except that there are no hornet or wasp keepers willing to take them for free.

I have had good luck using spray from a local hardware store. You spray the nest late at night or early in the morning. Then check for activity in a couple of days.

Another piece of advice, that I am not sure if it works or not, is to display a paper bag that look like it could be a wasp nest. I have been told wasps will not build a nest close to another one.

If you have rentals in an area prone to lots of insets that sting, you will want to find out if your tenants are allergic to stings. If they are, make sure they have an epie pen (in case they go into anaphylactic shock.)

Rats That Will Not Give Up

This is a story that happened a few years back in a single family home we rented to a couple. I received a call one day that there was a rat sighting in the house. The tenants seemed upset about the situation. I went to the house and set up some traps. About a week went by and I received a call from the tenant to say there was a foul odor coming from the closet that holds the water heater. I went to the house and found a rat in one of the traps I set. There I am standing outside the closet wearing a shirt and tie holding the trap with the rat in it, and I notice maggots falling on the floor. They were small maggots squirming around on the floor. Fortunately, I brought paper towels and plastic bags with me. I cleaned up the maggots, sprayed the area where I found the rat and left.

About two months went by and I received another call. More rats. I went to the house and this time I decided to educate the tenant on a few things that may deter rats from coming back. Number one, these tenants hardly ever mowed the lawn. That meant lots of long grass and areas for rats to hang out. They also were not the best at garbage storage. They had overflowing garbage cans (apparently, they had missed garbage day the week before).

I called my exterminator. He came out to set some traps. He also made some recommendations on areas around the foundation (crawl space) that the rats might be getting in. I had my handy-man come out and seal up any areas where I found holes. He also told me that rats don't like change. He said to move things around in the crawl space basement. That might be enough to freak out a rat and have them leave. The traps seemed to have worked. We haven't seen any more rats since that time.

Bed Bugs

Bed bugs are a recently growing problem. I want to share a second-party story on this situation. A property manager I know runs a continuing care facility that has several of its rooms subsidized by the government. That way, she can accept people of all economic levels. I don't want to suggest that this is just a problem for the poor. Anyone can get bedbugs. We also have a responsibility as a culture to work on eliminating bed bugs. My friend is very strict about when people move in. They have to have their belongings checked, because they've had a lot of expensive bed bug problems.

This story is about a tenant who moved in and snuck in some furniture late at night. As a result, the tenants below, above and side to side all ended up with bedbugs. When they went to inspect this particular tenant's apartment, she didn't want to let them in. When she finally agreed, it turned out she was a hoarder with an apartment full of bedbugs. This particular tenant caused a lot of grief for all the tenants around her, not to mention the expense. Bedbugs can be very difficult to get rid of if you want to save any furniture or clothes. It's important that your tenants don't bring in furniture from unknown sources. It's also important to check local bedbug building registries to make sure you aren't moving tenants in who are moving from infested buildings.

I would highly recommend you hire a professional who has a guarantee.

If you do end up with bedbugs, you can start by cleaning up the spots where they like to live:

Make sure to remove light switch and plug covers, spray behind them.

Clean sheets, blankets, pillows, curtains, and clothing in hot water. Dry them on the hottest setting. Put items that cannot be washed like stuffed animals and shoes in the dryer for 30 minutes.

Use a hard-bristled brush to scrub your mattress before you vacuum it to remove bedbugs and eggs.

Vacuum your bed and surrounding area. When you're done, place the cleaner bag in a garbage bag and put it outside.

Put a tight zippered cover over your mattress and box spring. Leave the cover on for at least one year (that is how long they can live without feeding). If your mattress is old, this might be a good time to replace it.

Make sure you remove any clutter from around your bed

Take a good look around the affected rooms and make sure to fill any cracks in the walls and glue down any peeling wallpaper.

I hope you don't have to deal with bedbugs, but if you do, it's good to know how to deal with them.

Raccoons Move into the Roof

This is a story about a family of racoons that took over a renovation project. We were replacing a roof on the back portion of one of our houses. The project involved removing the shingles, sheathing, soffit, and facia, and then rebuilding it.

We had the job almost complete and then left for the night. We didn't think about racoon squatters, so we left without covering the holes where the new soffit and facia was going to go on the next day. When the crew arrived and started working the next morning, they heard some funny noises. A family of racoons had moved into the attic, and they were not pleased about the construction crew bothering them.

We had to stop construction and over the course of the next few days, we were able to capture them all in live traps. We were able to release them all out into the wild. We then completed the job and sealed up the attic.

Raccoons can be quite a problem when you have properties. They love garbage and operate after dark. You cannot approach them because they can be quite vicious. If you don't have the proper traps, I would suggest using the services of a professional.

Should You Allow Pets to Occupy Your Rental?

We live in a world where people enjoy the company of pets, especially dogs and cats. There are also other kinds of pets such as fish, lizards, snakes, ferrets, spiders, and hamsters.

I'm often asked if I allow pets. I get this a lot from potential tenants. I feel if you allow certain pets, you can increase your competitive advantage. I also feel it's important to know the risks. I'll share some of my personal observations, and you can make your own decision.

At the time of writing this book, we consider pets on a case-by-case basis. We've had experiences with great pet owners, and several not so great pet owners.

164

The first broad observation is that everyone loves to have a pet if they can afford it or not. The decision to get a pet seems to be driven by emotion or circumstance. Maybe someone is giving away kittens or a puppy and the person gets caught up in the moment and doesn't consider the expense and responsibility of pet ownership.

Dogs – I've met both good and bad dog owners. One rule we have is the dog needs to be fixed and up to date with current vaccinations. We have a separate pet application and need to meet the dog before it moves in. We write a special clause in the lease that refers to eviction of the dog based on damage, barking, or any other nuisance complaints. We don't allow the dog to be left outdoors tied up for extended periods. The kinds of damage dogs can do include digging holes in the yard, chewing on stairs and doorframes, and scratching doors and floors. Also, if your tenant does no cleanup after the dog, it can leave quite a mess in the yard. It's important to make sure it's a friendly dog. You could be held liable if the dog were to attack a person while on your property. If you have a responsible dog-owning tenant, allowing dogs can give you a competitive advantage. Many people don't allow dogs at all. Our current opinion is that as long as you set the expectations, it can be fine to allow dogs in certain properties. In our area, dog ownership is not a protected human right; however, some blind people have guide dogs, and some older people are starting to claim that a small dog is for health reasons, claiming it's therapeutic.

Cats – Cats can be an okay pet to allow. You need to make sure the cat is fixed and up to date on its vaccinations. Cats can be quite destructive. Scratching things with its claws can cause a lot of damage. The biggest problem is cat urine. If a cat pees in your unit, that can be a major problem. It can soak right through a carpet and into the flooring. It can be very difficult to get rid of. Also, if your tenants are slack about cleaning the cat litter box, they can give off a very foul odor. They can also make noise and prompt noise complaints. That noise can be from a loud meow, or them running around late at night. The other problem is that, sometimes, people will like to collect cats. We allowed a lady to have two cats, and, a while later, we found out she had five. She didn't have enough money to look after herself. We told her she would have to leave or the cats would have to leave. She ended up getting rid of the extra three cats.

Aquariums – If you have a tenant who likes fish and wants to have a big aquarium. It may be okay to allow it, as long as there's not a lot of noise from the filter. Check with your insurance company to make sure it is okay to have a large aquarium in your rental property. The large aquariums hold a lot of water, so they can be a major problem if they leak or get knocked over.

Snakes – I've had a few tenants with snakes. I don't get the fascination, but some people really like them as a pet. I did hear in the news recently about a pet snake that killed a young boy. I've also heard stories of them escaping and not being found for days. I haven't had any bad experiences with snakes; however, I would put them on a maybe, case-by-case basis.

All other pets – I would recommend talking to your potential tenant about other pets. You'll need to consider the noise, smells, and liability if they cause harm to you or another person on your property.

CHAPTER 11 – EXPENSE REDUCTION

"Look everywhere you can to cut a little bit from your expenses. It will add up to a meaningful sum" – Suze Orman

In landlord/property management, the margins can be razor thin. If you're already charging rent at the top of market, you won't be able to increase revenue with rent increases.

To add to the pressure on your bottom line, water, electricity, natural gas, oil, propane, insurance, property tax, tenant turno-ver, capital repairs, and maintenance bills are always increasing and causing a negative impact on your bottom line.

The way to increasing your bottom line can often be as easy as watching your expenses and lost revenue.

Minimizing vacancy – This might seem obvious, but it really isn't. On average, you will have tenant turnover approximately every two years. You need to find out why people leave. Listen to your tenants. If you have outdated apartments, and new apartments get built close by for the same amount of rent, you could lose people to your competition. I can remember one situa-tion in particular when a simple conversation with a tenant in a building next to one we owned turned into getting a great tenant who stayed with us until they bought their own house. They were paying more money for a place half as nice. I just showed them our vacancy and the rest was history. Their landlord likely never even asked why they were leaving, but their being out of touch with the market was to my benefit. If you have a vacancy, fill it. You'll need to refer to chapter 2 for more information on filling your vacancy. However, in a nutshell, don't be lazy and fill it.

Charge the correct amount of rent – Know your market; charge accordingly.

Doing stuff yourself – Sometimes, it's cheaper to hire someone to do a job for you; however, if you have the skill to do a job properly and have the time to do it, it can save you cash. I will caution you to make sure you keep in mind what your time is best spent on. If you're out painting apartments and changing light bulbs instead of searching for your next deal, it could be a very expensive paint job.

Bank Fees – Bank fees can eat into your bottom line. Make sure you get a banking package that works for you. There are many options, especially when it comes to business banking. Keep an eye on these every month. Talk to the bank about your fees and how you can reduce them. Some banks will even charge money to cash checks and use bank machines.

Advertising/Marketing expenses – How much is it costing you to advertise a vacancy? Are there free options available? Should you be spending money to get your unit rented quicker? Are you sponsoring events just for ego to see your logo in public? Do you have a complicated expensive website that you don't need?

Have a maintenance schedule and stick to it – Sometimes, it costs more to repair something a couple of times than to replace it. I had a case once where I was trying to get one more winter out of a roof. I had to have my contractor do three patch jobs that winter. I ended up wasting close to $1,000 on repairs that had to be removed when we did the whole roof job in the spring. I should have bit the bullet that fall and had the whole thing done. I would have avoided three panicked calls from tenants and me to my contractor and saved $1,000 on the job.

Fuel – You'll need to do property drive-bys, so have a plan to maximize your use of time spent on the road. We have a specific route we use. The cost of fuel can add up. Also, what kind of vehicle are you driving? I've seen many people buy big gas-guzzling trucks, when in reality they could likely just use a car 99% of the time or a small truck. Keep a log of how often you need a truck. You can also buy a utility trailer to tow behind a small truck or car. Most building supply companies will deliver building supplies to job sites for you. If you have a truck with a plow, unless you're going to properly bill it as a business, you're better off hiring someone with a plow to do the work for you. I've seen many property managers and landlords driving gas-guzzling trucks that they don't need.

Building supplies – If you're buying a large amount of building supplies from one place, you can usually set up a credit account that will have a discount attached. This can make a big differ-ence to your bottom line. Also, if you're ordering a large quantity of supplies, most building supply places are willing to negotiate by offering a discount or some of the supplies for free.

Property management fees – Make sure you're getting good value for your dollar. Keep a close watch on the competition and make sure your property manager is always ready to provide a value proposition.

Heating / cooling costs – I think we have all driven by apart-ment building in the winter with open windows. If you're paying for heat in an apartment building or for any tenants, make sure to educate them on basic heat-saving measures, such as keeping the windows and doors closed, also turning the heat down at night and in the day when they're at work. Set up programmable thermostats. Install an outside thermometer that communicates with the furnace, to regulate the maximum temperature in a unit. You only need to heat to room temperature, so you can regulate the maximum temperature in your heated units. Also, make sure your buildings are properly insulated. Many old homes don't have any insulation in the walls. This is the same for air condi-tioning units on hot days. Educate your tenants on the effect of having windows open. If you have an air conditioner in a unit, make sure the the tenant knows how to use it.

Water – This is a continuously increasing expense. Many land-lords include cold water in the rent. The first thing you can do is see if you can arrange for your tenant to pay the water bill. If it's a multifamily, this may not be possible.

A second idea is to charge the regular market rent plus a water surcharge. This method is becoming more and more common in residential real estate, especially in areas where the cost of wa-ter is high. This might not cover your entire water bill, but it will help. Plus, it allows you to advertise your apartment for rent at the regular rate.

A third idea is to install low-flow shower heads, and low-flow valves on sinks. You can also replace your toilets with new ones that use significantly less water.

A fourth idea is to take a close look at your water bills for irregularities. I had a tenant go away for two weeks and left the bathtub tap on a trickle so the cat could drink. I noticed a high water bill and, after some investigating, the tenant confessed.

A fifth idea is continuous maintenance – When you do your routine maintenance inspections, look for water leaks, bathtub taps, sink taps, listen to drains, check for running toilets, check all visible pipes for leaks. I had a valve malfunction that was in the wall of a six-unit apartment building. When I stood in the laundry room, I could hear what sounded like water running into the floor drain. After some investigation, my plumber found the problem. He had to cut a hole in the wall and replace the valve.

Electricity/Hydro – We get our tenants to pay their own power bill in the majority of our units. We have a few exceptions of utilities included for older or fixed income tenants. The power company in our area will allow tenants to pay on a budget plan, in which they pay the same amount each month.

If you're paying for electric heat and cooling in a unit, I hope this advice will help save you money. Install programmable thermostats and set them up for your tenant. This is an easy way to save money, and your return on investment to pay for the programmable thermostats will be quick. Have your electric baseboard heaters inspected by an electrician; some of the older ones are not very energy efficient. Install heat pumps to complement the baseboard heaters. The heat pumps will also give your tenants air conditioning in the summer.

In your common areas, install sensors on your lights. That way, you don't have to rely on someone to turn them off in the day and on at night. Replace old appliances with newer, more energy-efficient appliances. You can also change your light bulbs to energy-efficient bulbs. If you have electric hot water heaters, put an insulated cover around them. You can have a maximum temperature gauge installed on your hot water heater or a timer, so you're not heating hot water 24 hours per day. Another system is called a thermal storage unit (a popular brand is called Steffes). When you install it, it will come with a time of day power meter, which will save you even more cash.

Another obvious way to reduce power cost is to keep a close eye on your power bills. If you see something unusual, then you may have an electrical problem, a grow op, or someone could be stealing power from you.

Natural gas – many people in our area have converted from oil to natural gas. The challenge came after the first year, when natural gas prices more than doubled. The good news from an expense reduction point of view, the government was offering rebates to people who were willing to convert to energy-efficient natural gas. The price can be relatively stable, and the maintenance cost of natural gas furnaces can be reasonably low. It can be a good expense reducer, but make sure to compare it to other heating systems. If you convert from oil to natural gas, you can save money on insurance by not needing pollution coverage.

Oil – getting away from oil heat can reduce expenses. It's interesting because, at the time of writing this book, the price of oil is at a historical low. The challenge with oil as a heating system is not just about the price of oil. The furnace and maintenance cost can be high, and the cost to insure yourself against leaks and pollution damage can be very high or not offered. The price of oil fluctuates, but can be very high. We've been converting all new acquisitions to a different heating source than oil.

Propane – Propane is comparable to natural gas and can be a great way to reduce expenses on heating and insurance costs. Also, a propane furnace can be easily converted to natural gas if you want to change it in the future. Make sure to do a cost comparison with whatever system you're changing from. You won't need pollution insurance as with oil systems, so you may have a savings on your annual insurance. You can also check for rebate programs that may save you money.

When you're managing properties, you need to keep track and analyze all your expenses on a regular basis. Any time you spend money, make sure it's a wise decision. The details can save you a lot of cash over the life of owning a property.

CONCLUSION

"Change favors the prepared mind." —Louis
Pasteur

If you've chosen the lifestyle of being a landlord/property manager, I hope you've found this book useful. Make sure you mark
pages and keep it as a manual to help if you get into a situation
that you're not sure about.

My wife and I are extremely passionate about the property management business and have met so many amazing tenants, real-
tors, other landlords, property managers, and contractors over
the years that it makes for a rewarding lifestyle. It is a lifestyle,
and it's not for everyone.

It has been very rewarding, and we do see some big returns financially, the current gains are being reinvested into the properties. One of the biggest rewards is being able to provide great
homes to great people.

It requires you to have thick skin, a pleasing personality, patience
of a saint, the willingness to work 24/7, problem-solving skills of
Einstein, and the ability to see the positive in every situation.

A good friend once told me there were no good situations or bad
situations, just situations.

I think my best advice to a new property manager/landlord is to
surround yourself with like-minded individuals. Get educated,
take a property management course, and join a real estate
group. If there aren't any in your area, you can join online.

I hope you enjoyed this book; if you have any feedback, I would
love to hear from you. You can reach me at landlord-
bydesign@gmail.com, Twitter: @michaelpcurrie or through the
following websites: www.landlordbydesign.com,
https://www.facebook.comlandlordbydesign,
https://www.linkedin.com/michaelcurriehalifax

ACKNOWLEDGEMENTS, SHOUT OUTS, AND CREDITS

"Nothing happens but first a dream" —Carl Sandburg

I want to recognize some of the great people who have helped me get to where I am today. It might have been through a business association, or a shoulder to cry on, when I had a tough day. I am so grateful to have met the following people.

These are all very special business people. Make sure you check out the websites of some of the folks who played a supporting role in my business.

The first shout out might be obvious, that's to my wife, Shelly Currie. She's also my property management/landlording partner. It's so amazing that I was able to find someone to share my business and life with. Thank you, Shelly for joining me on this amazing journey.

I want to shout out to our business partner and vice-president of The Fort Nova Group (our real estate investment company), Michael Thibeau.

I want to thank my dad, Don Currie and stepmother, Maureen Currie, who on more than one occasion have stepped in to help with various property management and cleaning jobs. Sometimes, we need all the help we can get to meet tight timelines.

Stefanie McDonald – has assisted me with some challenging tenant issues, and has provided me with amazing business advice: Halifax Paper Hearts – stefanie@halifaxpaperhearts.com

Egon Wallet – Palm Beach Properties – Egon has supported my real estate investing career and introduced me to Richard Payne's real estate investing group. wallet_egon@hotmail.com

Richard Payne – Keller Williams Realty – Multifamily investor and founder of The Halifax Real Estate Investors Meetup group – richard@richardpayne.ca, Richard@invictaproperties.ca

Scott Bentley and Igor Geshelin - The Bentley Group at Premiere Mortgage Centre. These two are responsible for finding the cash for all our projects. www.thinkBENTLEY.com

Patrick Johnston – serial entrepreneur, motivator
patrickmjohnston@gmail.com

Nick Harvey – always there for advice, very knowledgeable about the power of positive thinking. Realtor, property manager, founder of HRM real estate meet up nick.harvey@century21.ca

Selby Gossett – a realtor who knows how to hustle and gets deals done sgosset@remax-valley.com

Gail Boudreau – a realtor who is always ready to serve and goes above and beyond boudreaug@sutton.com

Christian Thibaudeau – Founder of ABC Property Management Ltd. A key property and project manager. My eyes on the ground 902-247-5918

Christian and Kim Thibaudeau: TCK Enterprises Ltd. Project and Investment property Consultants -
tckenterprisesltd@gmail.com

Keith Dexter – Serial entrepreneur, business mentor – makes complicated business problems look easy
kdexter@helmco.ca

Randy Stevens – Real estate investor, mentor – makes real estate investing look easy – jdrstevens@estlink.ca

John Copp – serial entrepreneur and friend – thank you for pushing me out of my comfort zone many times
john@creativecurvemedia.ca

Garnet Brooks – Lawyer, Internet marketer – the person who encouraged me to start a blog, and takes care of all our legal work. garnet@entrepreneurlaw.ca

Ian Knowles – General Contractor – let's just say we've been through a lot together – kconconstructionltd@hotmail.com

Edwin Maremont – Kore Construction, real estate entrepreneur – always there for advice and willing to help when I have serious maintenance issues – emarmont@gmail.com

Alex Jacobsen – Home Inspector – always ready to help – alex@novaspec.ca

Eric Wier – electrical contractor, we've run some serious wires together – erico.energy@live.com

John Pace – Pace Plumbing, always on call for us, no matter how busy they are: 902-477-4633

Derek Kaye – Internet Marketing guru – thank you for helping me navigate and open my eyes to networking, plus motivating me to write and publish this book: info@pushandpullmarketing.com

Kyla Cormier – Spiritual advisor – need I say more? kylacormier@hotmail.com

Drew MacQuinn – Hypnotist, meditation/mindfulness expert halifaxmindfocused@gmail.com

Tim and Brynn Blais – entrepreneurial power couple tim@gatewaybusinessbrokers.ca

Ed Nix – Insurance broker and educator of all things insurance enix@bellandgrant.com

Corey Poirier – Thank you for your encouragement, and helping me promote this book. http://thepassioncure.com/ https://youtu.be/TLBvm3DWgBU

Paul McInnis – Thank you for being a great sounding board for real estate investing ideas. pmacinnis@kes.ns.ca

David Campbell – Commercial real estate investor / Auto repair and sales / Business mentor e.harrington@hotmail.com

In addition, all the other people who played supporting roles in our real estate journey.

I cannot thank you enough.

Our most challenging renovation project

GLOSSARY

Cash Flow

Cash flow is the amount of money left over after all expenses are paid. It can be broken down by month, quarter, or year. A basic example is as follows: Rent (revenue) $1,500 Less Expenses Mortgage $800 insurance $200 property tax $150 Water $60 Lawn care $50 Maintenance $50 Total expenses $1,310

Rent (revenue) $1,500 minus Expenses $1,310 = a cash flow amount of $190 per month.

Class of buildings

Class A buildings are upscale. They compete for the higher income tenants. They will have rents that are above the average for the area. An A class building will also have the top of the line appliances for the area. Items like granite countertops and stainless steel appliances.

Class B buildings are average. They compete for tenants looking for nice clean rental space. A B class building would be in a good neighborhood. The rents would be at about average for the area. The finishes would likely be white instead of stainless steel.

Class C buildings are more functional or utilitarian. The units might be renovated, but would have basic appliances and cupboards. The rents would be below the average. C buildings are found in lower income areas.

Cosigner

The cosigner is a person that is liable for the terms and conditions of a lease, but does not live in the rented space. A cosigner must meet all the qualifying requirements of the landlord. They would be necessary if a person such as a student might not meet income, or rental history requirements to rent an apartment. They may also be necessary if and applicant does not meet credit rating requirements.

Customer Service

Customer service has three main components: communication, attitude, and relationships. It is about listening and providing your customers (tenants) what they want.

Damage Deposit

The damage deposit is an amount paid to the landlord when a lease is signed for any damages caused by the tenant. The damage deposit is kept in trust by the landlord for the duration of the lease. If the rented space does not have any damage after the tenant moves out, then it will be returned to the tenant. The amount you are allowed to collect (if any) is regulated by the local tenancy board. Another term for a damage deposit is *security deposit*.

Michael P Currie/Landlord By Design

Default

Default describes when a tenant does not pay the rent. They are considered to be in default.

Deadbeat

A tenant who does not pay rent

Deductible

A deductible is the portion of an insurance claim that the owner is responsible for. An example would be that if you had a sewer back up that cost $10000 in damages and you have a $5000 deductible, then the insurance company would pay the claim less the deductible. It would mean you get $5000. The deductible can be adjusted. You can save money on insurance by increasing your deductible, but you need to be prepared to bear the extra expense if you have a claim.

Eviction

Eviction is the legal process by which a tenant may be removed from a property due to violations of the terms and conditions of the lease. Reasons for an eviction could be for not paying rent, for operating an illegal business (such as dealing drugs) or for being a danger to other tenants in the building. The eviction process is based on the tenancy laws of a specific area.

Giving notice

Giving notice is when a tenant lets you know they will be leaving. Every lease should include a specified time period for when a tenant has to let you know they intend to leave. Another term for this is *Notice to quit*.

Landlord

A landlord is the owner. The person or corporation that has all or partial ownership of a building.

Lease

The lease is a signed agreement between landlord and tenant. There are several kinds of leases. A lease agreement contains a series of terms and conditions that are agreeable to landlord and tenant. Residential leases must be structured in a way to comply with local tenancy laws and regulations. Most government websites will have standard lease forms for residential leases. Commercial leases do not usually have many restrictions.

Lease up

The term lease up describes the process of getting signed leases in place on space that is available for rent.

Make Ready

A make ready is the process of getting a space ready for rent. A make ready could include anything from cleaning to a full renovation. A typical make ready would be a paint job, cleaning, and basic maintenance repairs (like a sticky lock).

Occupancy date

The occupancy date is the date that the tenants lease starts. On the occupancy date, the tenant will be required to have all required utilities hooked up in their name. The tenant may not move into the space on this date; however, the lease will begin.

Property Manager

The property manager is the individual or company that takes care of the daily operations of a property. They will also do or oversee activities such as making sure all spaces are cleaned and rented, and maintenance and repairs are taken care of. The property manager works for the landlord or, in a small operation, can be the same person.

Project Manager

A project manager is a person or company that oversees a specific renovation. The project manager will generally work under the guidance of the property manager or landlord. An example would be if you were going to renovate or build something, the project manager would arrange the trades people required such as a general contractor, electrician, and plumber. The project manager will keep a close watch on the progress of the work and make sure the project runs smooth. In many cases, a property manager may also offer the services of a project manager.

Renters' beige

Renters' beige is a paint color that can be used to paint all rented spaces. It is a non offensive color that appeals to most people. It can be manufactured by most paint companies, and the specific shade is not important as long as it is not too dark or too light. It should be purchased in 5-gallon buckets to maximize savings and allow you to always have enough on hand to paint a few units. Top quality paint is recommended, so you maximize coverage and cover imperfections in walls.

Rental income

Rental income is the amount of money you claim on your tax returns that you have collected from your rental properties. It is important to make sure to get proper tax advice and work with an accountant that is familiar with doing tax accounting for landlords. There are several tax benefits (in the form of expenses) to owning rental properties.

Revenue

Revenue is the gross amount of money you collect from your tenants. When you collect rent, it is considered revenue. It is the amount before expenses. A building could have a lot of revenue, but could have a very low or negative net income, once you deduct the expenses.

Roach

A roach is a potential tenant who has poor credit or lacks the credentials to rent an apartment

Security deposit

See "damage deposit"

Squatter

A squatter is a person or persons who reside in a space, but do not sign a lease or pay rent. It is more common to find squatters in abandoned buildings; however, they have been noted to show up in vacant space that is available for a paying tenant. Some areas have rights for squatters; you may have to follow an eviction process to get rid of them.

Tenant

The tenant is the person or company that occupies a rented space. They are the customer of the landlord/property manager.

Turnover

Turnover refers to when one tenant leaves and a new one moves in. It can be the most expensive part of owning rental properties.

Types of paint jobs

- **Deluxe** – a deluxe paint job is where the baseboards, trim, and ceiling are all painted white, and the walls are a different color.

- **Basic Paint job** – a basic paint job is where the ceiling is white and the trim and baseboards are the same color as the walls.

- **Quick and dirty** – a quick and dirty paint job is where the ceiling, walls, trim, and baseboards are all one color.

Vacancy

Vacancy refers to unoccupied space that is available for rent.

Vacancy rate

The vacancy rate is the estimated amount of unoccupied rented space in a particular area. If an area has a vacancy rate of 10% then you could count on one in every 10 units being vacant. It is important to monitor your buildings vacancy rate to the areas vacancy rate. The vacancy rate in most established areas is usually between 1 – 6%. Greater than 6% usually indicates and area with low population, too much rental supply, a depressed economy or a combination of several factors.

ABOUT THE AUTHOR

Michael Currie is a landlord and property manager from Canada. He had been flipping houses from 2001 until 2009 when he, his wife, and a close friend formed The Fort Nova Group Limited.

Since 2009, they have been using a buy/hold investing strategy, and, with the exception of a couple of income property flips, have been building an investment portfolio.

Michael has extensive experience working with contractors, trades people, project managers, property managers, and tenants to make renovations as non-disruptive as possible.

As soon as Michael got involved in buy and hold investing, he saw a need for property management education.

He started a mission to educate and assist independent landlords all over the world with his blog.

In addition to Michael's hands-on property-management experience, he and his wife, Shelly took a course on property management and are IPOANS CAM Certified (Certified Apartment Managers).

When Michael is not managing, buying, or helping people with properties, he enjoys spending time with family, boating, hiking, playing with cars, and helping to promote entrepreneurship.

landlordbydesign@gmail.com

Twitter: @michaelpcurrie

Instagram: @landlordbydesign

www.landlordbydesign.com

https://www.facebook.comlandlordbydesign

https://www.linkedin.com/michaelcurriehalifax

CPSIA information can be obtained
at www.ICGtesting.com
Printed in the USA
FSHW04n1951220318
46081FS